T0367291

Innovating Business Processes for Profit

How to run a process program for business leaders

Richard Stoneham

BALBOA.
PRESS

A DIVISION OF HAY HOUSE

Art Credit: Pippa Stoneham

Balboa Press books may be ordered through booksellers or by contacting:

Balboa Press
A Division of Hay House
1663 Liberty Drive
Bloomington, IN 47403
www.balboapress.com.au
1 (877) 407-4847

Printed in the United States of America.

ISBN: 978-1-4525-2660-7 (sc)
ISBN: 978-1-4525-2661-4 (e)

Balboa Press rev. date: 05/01/2015

CONTENTS

PROLOGUE

Many years ago I project managed a 'downsizing' for the company I worked for. Over a hundred people found they had lost their jobs by the time the project was completed. How were these unfortunate people picked? Essentially, the senior managers met in a room and nominated those who would go, without proof they were the right people, without any form of analysis of their work. I do give credit to the experiential judgement which many senior managers exhibit, so perhaps the right people were picked, but the result of this exercise was that over the next year or so, contractors and new employees were brought in to fill resource gaps and other employees worked excessive hours—because the amount of work had not decreased.

By the end of the year I was convinced there had to be a better way for an organisation to determine the right resourcing for the work it had to do and it had to find better ways of doing the work so that fewer people were needed. If that were possible, we would have avoided employing supposedly too many people in the first place, and consequently, avoided the misery of downsizing. What was needed was a method of finding the best work methods and the right numbers of people with the right skills to undertake that work. And we had to be able to prove we had the right numbers to resist arbitrary cost-cutting exercises; although, such macho decisions will undoubtedly continue to be made in some cultures.

I carried on in senior management roles and learned much about what it meant to take responsibility for business goals, strategies and problems. I did 'enterprise transformation' work and discovered that processes were behind all work undertaken by any enterprise. That seems obvious, but typically, organisations did not actually think that way. At that time there were Quality Departments that defined these processes, but they were typically working at far too low a level to interest senior management and so were disconnected from strategic thinking.

I worked on major processes. The organisation I worked for was spending large amounts of money on bidding for large contracts and the number of wins was so low that the organisation was considering ways of reducing bid costs. What it really needed to do was avoid unsuccessful bids but it was in danger of reducing good bids as well. So we worked on the bid process and people got excited by what we did. The result was fewer bids and just as many wins, so we avoided spending a lot of money.

The key to this success was working at a high enough level that stakeholder business managers could identify with what was going on, and consequently produce really clever ideas for redefining the process. This was process innovation, not just improvement. And so I learned to differentiate between the business activity level, which business stakeholders could easily relate to, and the task or procedural level, which was really only of interest to the people who did specific tasks—and at the task level few people took an interest (or were encouraged to take an interest) in the whole process.

Process innovation is done at the activity level, further improvements are made later at the task level when procedures are defined but the benefits of process innovation—in terms of improved customer service and resource savings—are much more important than the benefits of the improvements.

I find today that few organisations understand this simple principle. The domination of information technology (IT) leads participants to focus on business requirements for the IT systems, and business requirements are necessarily written at the task level. And so the opportunity to innovate processes at the business activity level is often missed. Many will deny this, citing the different levels of process analysis, but my observation is that the time pressure on large IT system projects results in a rush to the business requirements stage and process innovation is, at best, sporadic and dependent upon the talents of skilled individuals.

Some senior leaders think processes are something to do with quality and need to be defined by operational managers and are therefore not of strategic importance. This is because they have not seen process work done above the task level. With generational change amongst business leaders they have come to realise business processes are strategically important, but they do not necessarily know how processes are best designed—they have to rely on others to manage this for them.

The IT industry recognised that business was looking for process solutions that would reduce resource costs, and over the last couple of decades has developed a new class of applications called Business Process Management Systems (BPMS) which deliver people-centric process automation and workflow management. Included in BPMS suites are tools for process analysis, but the previous point applies— although BPMS allow process analysis at multiple levels, the emphasis is on getting to business requirements at the task level, which form the instructions for the system configuration.

I believe there is a need for senior business leaders to understand how to own and lead process programs in order to deliver process innovation, which generates significant business benefits. This book is for those senior executives and aspirational managers in service organisations who need to lead successful process programs. It is an area of expertise that is a key driver for excellence in organisational management.

The phrase 'for profit' is used in the book title. This does not limit the relevance of the book to leaders in commercial organisations, the phrase 'for organisational gain' is equally applicable for government, educational and not-for-profit organisations. Indeed at the time of writing there is great focus on process work in such organisations, and the benefits for them are considerable.

There are some very erudite business process management books available in the market. However, they are intensive and more likely to be read by Business Process Management (BPM) professionals. The intent of this book is to provide a more accessible source for busy executives and managers who are interested in BPM, but only as one aspect of their responsibilities, and who need enough understanding to be able to own and manage BPM programs effectively. At the same time, there is practical guidance and templates in this book to enable managers to set up and run BPM projects within a BPM program.

I want to emphasise that whilst IT systems are often used to supposedly implement processes, what they really often do is implement tasks or functions, not end-to-end processes. Computer systems are not processes, they are merely the tools for implementing processes. Books about process design are often written from an IT viewpoint and I believe that is the wrong starting point. I don't wish to denigrate or diminish IT, it is vitally important to the modern enterprise, but my concern is to ensure that the IT system implements the best processes for the organisation.

This book does discuss how business people should interact with IT people and Business Process Management Systems (BPMS), but it is not a book about technical IT work or the BPMS technologies as such.

Having said that, I know that business analysts and IT leaders can learn much from this book about how their clients think, or perhaps should think.

The book is divided into eighteen chapters (see Index). Senior leaders can skip some chapters, leaving them to their project leaders. At the same time the book can be dipped into as necessary, however I encourage the reader to read the first two chapters before jumping into later chapters.

Richard Stoneham
November 2014

CHAPTER 1

Strategic Considerations — Supporting the Business

Business processes are the business; they are how an organisation delivers products or services to its customers. Without processes there is no basis for a commercial business or public service. A business leaders' and managers' job is to ensure processes are designed and implemented that enable the organisation to deliver the right product or service to the customer at the right level of quality and customer value in the most efficient and cost-effective manner. Products or services need differentiation and credibility in the market, customer experience and perception of value are crucial to an organisation's reputation and survival.

What do we mean by 'process'?

You may say, 'We know what a process is'. But do you? The real meaning of 'process' is the end-to-end stream of activities[1] that

---

[1]   An activity is a sequence of tasks that create an interim output or change of state, for example, the activity 'receive customer order' results in an interim output—the order, or a change of state—order received. An activity merely states what happens, not how it happens.

finish with delivery of value to the customer and reach back across the organisation to encompass all activities that contribute to that outcome, without regard to functional boundaries. Yet most 'processes' in organisations are defined within a function.

Scientific management has taught us to optimise the function we manage. Our careers are built on functional excellence. But what is optimal for a function is not optimal for the organisation as a whole. Indeed, a lot of wasted resource and cost, frustration, and political infighting are caused by this paradigm. Processes, on the other hand, are based on the idea that we need to optimise for the whole organisation and all participants contribute to the value created for the customer.

What a process is

Here are two definitions of process from renowned management authors:

'A process is simply a structured, measured set of activities designed to produce a specified output for a particular customer or market.' [i]

'Process: an organised group of related activities that together create a result of value to the customer.' [ii]

'A result of value' is a crucial aspect of any process output. If an output is not one of value to a customer why is it being performed at all? This question is important in testing process designs.

In this book 'process' means an end-to-end group of business activities that produces outputs of value to the customer. However, it can also mean activities producing outputs of value to the organisation in supporting and managing outputs of value to its customers; these are secondary, or support, processes. Note that it does not matter where in the organisation a process starts or ends, functional boundaries are not inhibitors to workflow

What a process is not

People talk about 'process' all the time, but are often referring to sub-processes or activities; that is, the parts of processes. In the process management context it is important to use 'process' in the broader sense so that the right result is achieved.

Processes do not include procedural detail. We will consider tasks[2] when we come to business requirements but before then we will only be describing business processes as comprising activities.

A process does not define job responsibilities, only how an individual or group contributes to the process outcome by completing activities. Job descriptions tend to talk about tasks, role descriptions about activities. The words are often treated as synonymous, but they are different.

What a process does

A process is a guide; it lends clarity to who does what, why, and in what order, but it does not specify how. It enables people involved in the process to understand their contribution to the customer outcome and how value is added, and accordingly, is about collaboration

---

[2] Tasks are about how a piece of work is done technically or by way of skill or expertise. A task is a piece of functional work, its definition includes 'how to' and is technically specific. 'Complete order form 123' is a task, as it states how to enter the order into a system. 'Complete order form 123' is also procedural, as it provides detailed instruction.

rather than the 'pass the parcel' behaviour common in functionally structured organisations.

Strategic drivers

Processes have been worked on for many years, particularly in the manufacturing sector, but in the modern service economy they have re-emerged as critical because of long-term strategic drivers, some of which are:

The rise of individuality in modern, middle-class, educated populations means services need to be tailored to the individual.

Customisation has superseded mass production or standard services, or rather modified them, for competitive advantage or the credibility of public organisations. Customisation means there are options and decisions as the process progresses. Commonly these are solved by human logic. However, as processes become more complicated and as different people may deal with options and decisions, inconsistencies creep in. Processes enable customisation with consistency.

Information explosion has led to a demand for flexibility of product or service. More and more information builds up in modern organisations. Information technology both supports this and causes this build-up. Processes are good at sorting which information is relevant for each activity.

Need for speed necessitates decision making on the spot, that is, immediate local decision making vs central decision making. This generates the need for guidelines to ensure decisions are made according to policy and strategy. This is a governance issue, if processes are not clear, the front-line people will not wait for a decision but will act as they see fit. To make the right decision they need to be adequately informed by the process, otherwise outcomes may be incorrect.

Improving quality is a means of promoting brand or reputation, which enables premium pricing or improved funding, which leads to growth in profit or political importance. Processes are essential to quality improvement.

Cost pressures arise due to increasing competition, or just keeping up with competition. Processes help reduce costs by removing the need for supervision; reducing rework and corrective actions; using the quickest method; enabling fast track options for some instances; simplifying by removing over-engineering; improving information flow; and perhaps other reasons.

Globalisation of markets with the internet, ecommerce and sophisticated information systems has resulted in increased competition, and opportunities. Organisations have to be better at what they do or they do not survive. Process is one critical way of getting better at what they do.

Rapid change with shorter and shorter product or service life cycles mean adaptability has to be built into systems and methods. Processes can easily be adapted at the activity level. There is more work at the task level but clarity at the activity level ensures this work is minimised.

Need for confidence in governance. Boards and executive teams need to be assured that governance systems are adequate and effective. Processes are a key instrument of governance as they provide guidelines and boundaries within which people do their work.

Complexity has resulted in central planning and control no longer working. Organisations are still trying out different organisational models but those that enable local decision making with central leadership and policy-making appear to be on the right track. The more local decision makers are informed, the greater the level of complexity that can be handled by an organisation.

These strategic drivers are the concern of top management, which must come up with strategies to stay alive and grow. It is incumbent upon senior management to ensure processes are in place so that decisions can be made locally according to policy, strategy and values, whilst not adding to overhead costs.

However, there must be a real business case for a process program, it must contribute to the organisation's long-term goals and provide a financial return.

Why spend valuable time on processes?

Whilst there may be IT software and infrastructure costs, the largest cost is the opportunity cost of management and staff time required to undertake a strategic process program. Management and staff time available to spend in change teams is a scarce resource. Process programs must support the organisational goals and strategies in order to gain management commitment and synergistic outcomes. These are some of the outcomes of process programs that are likely to be strategic objectives.

Business reasons for a process program

1) Creates strategic advantage
   - Enables operationalisation of business strategy
   - Improves customer perception of value

- Reduces business risk
- Provides governance framework

2) Promotes operational efficiency
   - Reduces cycle time
   - Enables local decision making
   - Reduces need for supervision
   - Increases resourcing flexibility
   - Frees up resources for other work
   - Reduces resource consumption costs
   - Provides opportunities for fast track options
   - Communicates clearer expectations
   - Reduces up-the-line referrals
   - Acts as operational checklist

3) Improves quality of output
   - Outputs are more predictable
   - Ensures consistency of outputs
   - Ensures requisite output quality
   - Provides baselines for further improvement and facilitates continuous improvement

4) Supports growth
   - Provides additional growth capacity, leads to more throughput, leads to greater revenues
   - Avoids future growth costs
   - Encourages repeat business
   - Facilitates planning and estimating activities
   - Improves reputation and referrals to acquire new business
   - Provides synergistic opportunities in other aspects of the business

5) Encourages a collaborative culture
   - Shows participants how they contribute
   - Encourages collaboration
   - Reduces internal conflict

- Enables better levelling of resources
- Improves staff satisfaction

All of these reasons contribute to improved profits by increasing revenues and reducing costs, they also contribute to the flexibility and sustainability of the business.

Background concepts

There are certain ideas and concepts that provide insight when considering processes. An understanding of these will enable executives to better appreciate the role of processes and how they fit into the strategic framework of any organisation, and enable them to ensure that the best is obtained from process programs they may own or in which they have a stake. What follows are introductions to these ideas and concepts, any that catch your attention are worthy of further reading and references are included in the bibliography.

Systems thinking — a holistic perspective

Systems thinking was applied to business in popular management theory with the publication of Peter Senge's 'Fifth Disciple'.[iii] He defines a system as, 'A perceived whole whose elements "hang together" because they continually affect each other over time and operate toward a common purpose'.[iv] The essential point of systems thinking is that everything is connected to everything else, and systems are:

- Dynamic
- Inherently stable
- Complex

- Cannot be divided without loss of characteristics
- Have emergent properties that seem to come out of nowhere
- May be counterintuitive
- Are fractal in nature (have systems within systems, within systems ...)

By way of example, project management is a discipline that traditionally operates by breaking down actions into lower levels of task then managing the tasks. This leads to system errors, for example, a project overruns, resources are added, the project gets even more behind at greater cost. There are many examples in the press of project overruns and cancellations costing millions of dollars. What is happening is that because the projects are being run at task level, system effects are not anticipated and the exactness of plans are lending a false sense of control whereas complex systems need a more sense-making approach and a greater sensitivity to change and interconnectedness. The systems effects in this example are 'unintended consequences' (a phrase that crops up regularly in politics because of a lack of understanding of systems thinking!). Simplistically, what happens with the addition of resources to the project is that communications, planning, training and management time goes up, involving many project members, and the overall overhead time increase is greater than the additional direct resource time.

Processes are systems, operating within systems, and need to be seen as having the characteristics listed above. Not only does the internal linking of processes and IT system implications need to be considered but it is also worth considering impacts and opportunities in other business areas, such as organisation structure; people classifications and rewards; financial management; legal risks; policies; regulations; and so on.

Theory of constraints (TOC) — organisational optimisation

TOC is an application of systems thinking.

Professional managers build their careers on functional skills and knowledge, they are trained to optimise the output of their functions, and their careers depend upon it.

TOC points out that at the enterprise level the output of the organisation as a whole is no greater than that of the most constrained department or function, given that there is a connected flow through the organisation. This is common sense but many managers ignore it and focus on their own unit's output. The net result is that:

-   Extra output in non-constrained units is useless, and the cost of improvement is wasted
-   Extra output in non-constrained units adds to system pressure as the constrained unit's output has not changed
-   Spare capacity is inevitable in non-constrained activities (it will not show because work increases or slows down to fill the time available)

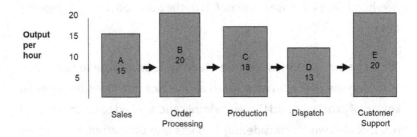

In the example above, the output of the organisation is constrained by Dispatch and cannot exceed 13 per hour. Expanding production output to 20 will not change the organisation's output; it will just increase pressure on Dispatch to no avail, and also on Sales and Order Processing to feed Production's new capacity.

With these insights TOC [v] suggests:

- Throughput is the real objective
- Identify the constraint to throughput
- Put effort where it affects end output, at the constraint, get all you can out of the constraint
- Any spare capacity should be directed at the most constrained activity, subject to skills
- Develop a culture that supports asking people to help with the bottleneck
- Invest in the constraint
- When the constraint is no longer the constraint, start over again with the new constraint

This helps when considering which processes to work on: identify and focus on the constraint area. To do this requires an understanding of how the flow connects through the organisation, that is, the end-to-end processes and how the processes fit into an overall process architecture for the organisation (more on this later).

Adaptive systems and evolution

Nature has developed mechanisms over millennia to arrive at how organisms function today. Any natural system has proved itself to be an optimum system by the process of evolution. Natural systems typically have structure within which there is a pattern of organisation in which everything connects, and there is a process of life.[vi] There is continual change and renewal within the organism so that an organism such as the human body is highly complex, dynamic, relatively stable, and functions effectively; it displays all of the characteristics of a system.

Examining how nature functions may give us insight into system design.

What lessons can we learn from nature? There are many, but to name a few:

- Everything within the overall organism is connected and inter-dependent
- Each organ has a distinct function within the overall structure
- Cells communicate through semi-permeable membranes enabling coordination
- Evolution depends on the symbiosis or collaboration between cells
- Evolution displays both gradual change and sudden spurts to achieve defensive or offensive gains

It is this pattern of dynamism, inter-connectedness, complexity and communication that offers insight into how modern complex organisations can survive and grow, rather than become inflexible, grow stale and die. Horizontal communication, such as between cells, and by analogue between people, enables flexibility and rapid response. The operation of processes provides knowledge of what to do, how to react, which contributes value and is akin to the life process. Continual refreshing and improvement is a survival mechanism and is dynamic. The sudden changes brought on by process innovation programs are like the spurts of evolution.

The process approach offers not just efficient function but also dynamic flexibility and adaptation. It adopts the same strategies as nature itself; in particular, a dynamic system approach that avoids the pitfalls and inefficiencies of a traditional hierarchical approach by allowing rapid horizontal communication and decision making within process guidelines.

Complexity theory

Before considering the implications of complexity theory on process programs it is important to understand certain terms.

Uncertainty: a state of having limited knowledge where it is impossible to exactly describe the existing state, a future outcome, or more than one possible outcome. For example, if you do not know whether it will rain tomorrow, then you have a state of uncertainty.[vii]

Certainty: the opposite of uncertainty, where enough knowledge is available to exactly describe the existing state or future outcome. Perfect computer systems produce certainty. Is that true? Well, probably not, because inputs are uncertain. As Voltaire said, 'Doubt is not a pleasant condition, but certainty is absurd.'

In practical terms, processes are intended to move an operational transaction closer to certainty from a state of uncertainty, but there will always be uncertainty, primarily because of the involvement of people.

A more useful distinction is made between complicated and complex.

Complicated: a condition which involves many connections with current uncertainty of outcome, but which can be worked through using known methods so as to predict the outcome accurately. Engineering and architectural designs deal with complicated tasks.

Complex: a condition in which the number of connections is so large that it is impossible to accurately predict outcomes. When engineering or architectural designs fails it is because the situation was in fact complex rather than complicated. Weather forecasting is complex, predictions are made but the outcome is never certain.

So, 'complexity relates to the number of relationships between the components, and complexity *rises geometrically* with the increase in the number of relationships'.[viii]

Given that organisations are a form of systems, within which everything ultimately connects to everything else, they are complex environments.

'Relationships and component behaviour are not predictable in the way we assume. In the face of complexity rigid planning tends to fail, as it cannot account for the large number of variations from expected behaviours and outcomes. To plan a system exactly it would be necessary to model all possible behavioural responses to each activity, and then each outcome is applied to the next activity, etc. This is an impossible task.' [ibid]

Modern organisations face great complexity; to try and *control* centrally is impossible. Managing complexity requires *leading* from the centre by providing strategies and objectives (direction), policies, infrastructure, physical assets, training and education. Processes are infrastructure. It is impossible to direct operations from the centre effectively; once the business environment is adequately provided and maintained by leaders then people are enabled to get on and do their work locally within the business framework that has been provided. It needs all of the people available to maintain all of the relationships inside and outside of an organisation—a network communications model is needed, not a pyramid model. Complexity in all aspects of life, including business, can only be handled by networked systems.

One of the observations in complexity theory is that evolution is maximised at the edge of chaos. It is easy to misapply what is a mathematical and evolutionary observation, but it has to be said that a little chaos is necessary to push a team away from the old way of thinking about a process—through the tipping point to a new way of thinking so as to innovate the process. This analogy is useful when faced with a workshop in disarray over the best solution! Work through the chaos. Look for new patterns and a better way will emerge!

Supporting management strategies

Leadership

Leadership is a term often used in modern organisations, and frequently misused. In this context the intended meaning of leadership is to point the direction towards a goal and inspire people to work together to achieve that goal. This is in contrast to management, which is about oversight of defined transactions and improvement of those transactions.

There are many different theories of leadership[ix], amounting to different styles, but our concern is to ensure that a process program has effective leadership to ensure change takes place. The style will vary by organisation and individual.

The leader does not design the change, which is up to the program team, but represents the program to the organisation and facilitates its completion.

People are naturally territorial and process programs do arouse territorial instincts. Without adequate leadership those who oppose a proposed change in process will be able to drown out the process team's proposals, and the program will fail. Even if process changes appear to be successful, opposition may arise when it becomes obvious organisational changes are implicit. Strong leadership from the top is required to resolve the tension between the functional, operational and process management camps. This is discussed further in the change management chapter.

Knowledge management and organisational learning

Knowledge management is the planning, organising, motivating, and controlling of people, processes and systems in the organisation to ensure that its knowledge-related assets are improved and effectively employed[x]. Organisational learning is the acquisition of knowledge on behalf of the organisation, based on experience.

Knowledge in peoples' heads and on personal hard drives or in paper files is called 'implicit'. Knowledge available to the organisation as needed is called 'explicit'. Good process design provides organisational learning by making implicit knowledge explicit, so that anyone can use the new process if they have the necessary technical skills. Once the process is implemented, ways of improving it become obvious, and ongoing process improvement becomes the second stage of organisational learning.

The ability for an organisation to constantly learn, improve and restructure to meet its goals in a changing environment is essential for survival. Without such adaptability, one day it will find it has been left behind.

Program management, project management and portfolio management

Program management is a business discipline which bridges between strategic planning and project implementations. Project management manages the implementation of change to the point where it becomes operational. Portfolio management balances the competing resource and time demands of programs and projects. Chapter 2 contains more explanation of these three business management disciplines.

It is not enough to just launch individual process projects. Business leaders need to own the program which contains process projects and manage the portfolio of projects. Only this way will the complexity of the organisation be adequately managed so that projects can succeed. There are too many project failures and one of the fundamental reasons is the lack of overarching program management. Often, the reasons cited for project failures are in fact symptoms whereas program management can provide a fundamental solution.

IT systems development

Some history

The information technology industry is staffed with clever people and some years ago they recognised that business people were rebelling against IT people telling them that what they needed to do was conform to IT vendor's application designs, and web technology was demonstrating the advantages of flexibility.

Business leaders had gone through generational change and had come from not having a good knowledge of IT to one of having a reasonable understanding of what IT could offer, and IT had moved from being just operational to becoming strategic for organisations.

The IT industry leaders had developed their market positions based on database technology, which requires users to know what to do next and call up the appropriate function or screen. Business leaders were grappling with complexity and reduced management levels and wanted technology to support workflow, which would manage processes dynamically and prompt the user with what to do next.

New IT companies sprung up, offering workflow management products. In due course, the database vendors saw the opportunity and started buying up the workflow management fledglings and incorporating them into their own product ranges. Gradually, these products became more and more complicated and the new name 'Business Process Management' emerged and the inevitable three letter acronym 'BPM' sprung into use and 'BPMS' (BPM Systems) became the acronym for these systems.

BPMS have enabled the IT vendors to seize the initiative to some extent, and they are promoting BPMS as the way to develop new processes.

Business and IT

The right place to start is with the business need and business process design. IT systems are tools, not the main purpose. They are very valuable tools, but they are still just tools. Because of the IT emphasis many so-called process projects are in fact IT system projects and fail to develop the best processes for the organisation.

Many IT system projects computerise an improved version of current work methods. This occurs because business management unwittingly abdicate their responsibilities and allow IT to own and drive IT projects. That is not IT's fault, it is business management's fault.

Having said that, IT is a powerful tool and what needs to happen is that a strong working relationship is forged between the business and IT people in any process project. However, business has to take the lead to get the best of the opportunity and IT Systems Development needs to respond to the process design. The development of IT systems business requirements should be done collaboratively, but the business owns the procedural content.

Quality management — the drive for excellence

Processes and quality have long been associated with each other. The quality movement was important in the latter part of the last century but suffered setbacks due a faulty organisational strategy:

organisations appointed Quality Managers, allowing the operational managers to 'pass the buck' to the Quality Manager and reduce the importance of quality in day-to-day management.

Whilst the International Organization for Standardization (ISO) certification remains important in certain technical industry and government domains, the concept of Excellence Frameworks has become more important for modern organisations. Public organisations and specific industries (e.g., health, energy, and pharmaceuticals) are the primary users, but the concepts apply to any business. Processes appear in most excellence models, here is the *European Excellence Model, revised 2012*[xi]

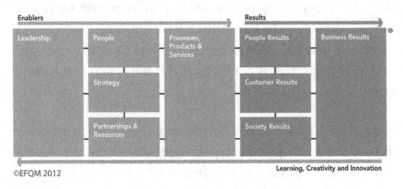

©EFQM 2012

Reproduced with EFQM permission.

The US *Malcolm Baldridge Awards* program contains a clear model for attainment of process maturity, which is shown below.[xii] This is useful for assessing where an organisation is on its process journey.

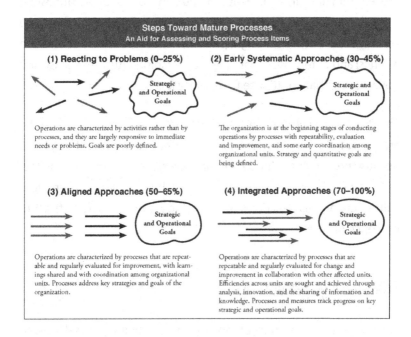

This figure is used with the permission of the Baldrige Performance Excellence Program. 2013. *2013–2014 Criteria for Performance Excellence.* Gaithersburg, MD: U.S. Department of Commerce, National Institute of Standards and Technology. Obtain a copy of the full Criteria at www. nist.gov/baldrige/publications/criteria.cfm.

Note that maturity is about process alignment with strategic and operational goals.

Where does your organisation fit on this scale?

Finally, Michael Hammer became well known as a business author and consultant during the Business Process Reengineering (BPR) era of the 1980s and 90s but continued to contribute to business process thinking until his death in 2008. In April 2007 he published a seminal article in the Harvard Business Review (HBR)[xiii] in which he cited process enablers (design, performers, owner, infrastructure and metrics) and enterprise capabilities (leadership, culture, expertise and governance) that contribute to maturity level.

The Process and Enterprise Maturity Model is expanded upon in the article but it underlines the organisational commitment required, because processes are fundamental to excellence in business. Indeed, the completion of a process program may be used to drive beneficial culture change as described above, which is notoriously difficult to influence directly.

Achieving high performance

The strategic drivers, concepts and management disciplines discussed in this chapter help explain and support what a process program should be about. It is too easy to approach a process program as a simple process mapping exercise. Indeed it is not uncommon for BPM to be thought to mean 'Business Process Mapping'. It does not mean that, it means 'Business Process Management', and BPM is about managing the business and requires high-level thinking, or a major opportunity will be lost—and what is worse; what is lost will never be understood to have been lost.

The opportunity is to secure the outcomes listed above in 'Business reasons for a process program'. These can fundamentally improve the customer experience and the efficiency of the organisation and enable the organisation to stand out as a high achieving business performer within its sector.

A process program is a key part of any strategic change initiative. Here are a few of the reasons.

- To undertake organisational restructure without a good understanding of workflow is to act without properly connecting work patterns to the superstructure.
- Driving culture change requires people to change how they work—using processes.
- Reforming governance needs good processes that define rules and limits.
- Assessing returns on capital investments needs knowledgeable costing of resource consumption—using process activity analysis.
- Driving improved revenue needs optimised operating processes to support additional throughput.
- Reducing costs effectively needs a method of changing practices so as to need less work, rather than just squeezing resource consumption

Processes are at the heart of strategic gains that lead to a stand-out organisation.

CHAPTER 2

Managing the Process Program — Implementing the Strategy

Program management

The purpose of program management is to deal with uncertainty and complexity. It is about sense-making, finding the way, developing islands of certainty, flexibility and adaptation. It manages overall implementation of the business strategy and realisation of the intended business benefits. Program management is a responsibility of business management.

On the other hand, project management is about delivery of individual implementation projects and to succeed there needs to be a certainty of objectives; a clarity of method, performance and delivery; and adjustment to program requirements. Programs will include multiple projects

Projects sit within programs; the following diagram illustrates the relationship. The numbered circles are projects, the overall rectangle is the program:

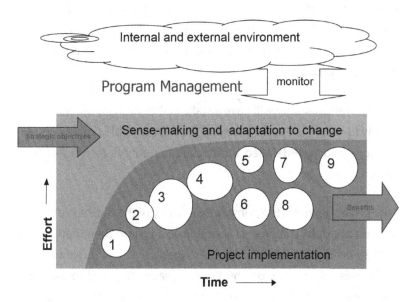

Organisation

The strategy that a program springs from is owned at the highest executive levels of an organisation. A meeting of an Executive Management Group (EMG) responsible for all strategies will appoint a Stakeholder Management Group (SMG) for each program which then selects and appoints a Program Owner, preferably one of the group members.

The Program Owner needs to decide on the fundamental principles of project team organisation and answer the questions below and report back to the SMG. It is a program function to make these strategic project organisation decisions.

Who will lead projects?

A good principle for process projects is to appoint business managers as Project Leaders rather than appointing professional Project Managers. Ideally, the business manager should be the person who most benefits from the operational improvements brought about by the process project.

The business manager will have a stake in the business outcome and is likely to ensure the team produces the best possible process design solutions and well-detailed business requirements for the process system.

If the project leader is the primary beneficiary of the business benefits brought about by the process redesign and system then that person may go on to become the process owner when it is implemented. Again, this will encourage the Project Leader to develop the best possible solution. Moreover, the Leader is best placed to sponsor any necessary changes in policy that may be required to implement the new process design and operation of the new process.

Should the project team be full-time or part-time?

It is often assumed that project teams should be full-time. This is not always the best principle. If people are used part-time then those who are in key roles can be included in the team whilst they maintain their normal role. This increases the chances of innovation and good design because the team members have the best knowledge. The team can meet for two or three hours a week or a fortnight in workshop, this level of participation can usually be absorbed by the team members.

In order to make this approach work, certain key people need to put in more hours to progress work between workshops—these will be the BPM specialist or consultant; an IT manager or analyst during the business requirements phase; IT developer(s) during the system configuration/development phase; a communications specialist, and any project support people as required.

If a project is to have a full-time team, people have to leave their normal roles. The first issue is that this may mean the best people cannot be released to participate in the project; moreover, the people assigned may not be the best people to represent their domain. Over time, the team develops a project culture based on the project imperatives and members start to diverge from their previous attitudes towards a new team perspective. This reduces their usefulness as stakeholder representatives as their origin departments perceive they have 'changed sides' and insist that their needs are not being taken into account. And so conflict develops, which makes development of processes and business requirements much harder.

The idea that a full-time team will develop a solution more quickly has some truth but surprisingly not in proportion to the extra resource time. A part-time team has gaps between workshops and this tends to lend greater clarity to what is being developed so many time-consuming cul-de-sac conversations do not get started.

The overall progress rate of the program may not vary much; a full-time team will often deal with one process at a time unless the project team is very large whereas a part-time team approach will enable multiple teams to work on multiple processes in parallel—so that more people will be involved for less individual time.

Finally, full-time teams necessitate marginal costs in providing backfill resources for their normal roles.

Ultimately, the basis of decision will be particular to the organisation's circumstances, but there must be a compelling reason to adopt a full-time team approach.

What about project management?

IT projects are typically managed by professional Project Managers. If the Project Leader is a business person, will there be adequate project management discipline applied to the project? This is an important question in terms of the expectations of management stakeholders.

IT projects are prone to failure—just read the business press—and the reason is that project management works on a principle of disaggregation and management of individual tasks. This works fine when there is clarity of method and objective, which is the case during the IT configuration/development phase. However, when there is uncertainty of objective, in that, the eventual process design is not known at the start, then complexity rises—bringing system effects into play—and project management just does not operate well at the system level.

So, whilst the IT development might benefit from tight project management, it actually discourages process innovation and good design, even during the business requirements phase.

What works well in practice is setting loose target dates for the process work and business requirements and managing these in a way that does not stifle innovation at a critical moment. Moreover, if a part-time team is used, budget is not an issue because there is no marginal cost for the team members, other than perhaps a BPM specialist deployed to the project from the program team.

'Light' project management tasks can be done by a member of the program team.

Project management

The purpose of project management is to deliver a change to the point where it becomes operational. Project management is not good at dealing with complexity, this needs to be handled at the program level.

Projects are much more successful when they have certainty and their duration is kept to the minimum. It is the program's function to provide the certainty and to launch multiple smaller projects rather than large monolithic projects. Certainty comes out of the sense-making stream and projects are initiated by the program team:

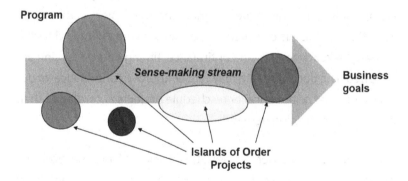

For the effective implementation of processes a strong distinction should be drawn between the process program and process projects. It is the direct responsibility of senior management to ensure the program is well sponsored, run and supported.

Project Management is a well-developed discipline and there are many specialised books available on the subject so its practice is not detailed here. However, we will look into the project management roles that the program appoints. We will spend more time on program management as that is where senior leaders need to focus.

Portfolio management

Portfolio Management of process projects is undertaken by the program leadership. Decisions about project funding, resourcing, initiation, continuance and variation are made according to priority, resource availability and strategic objectives as they change over time.

Prospective projects are added to the portfolio as they are identified and the portfolio management process will take them though several steps until they are approved. Once approved, a project may await key resources before being initiated. Upon initiation, key project personnel are appointed, resources are assigned and the project commences. Each time a phase is completed or a 'gateway' (meaning a decision gateway) is reached, project continuance, timing and resourcing are reviewed. The portfolio team may cancel, approve continuance (or put conditions on continuance) or reschedule projects according to their merits and competing demands.

There may be a higher, organisational level of project portfolio management covering multiple programs, to which individual program leaders may report, so that resource deployment is optimised across the organisation.

Roles and responsibilities

When looking at roles it is important to understand the stages of a process program, each of which has its own roles and responsibilities:

Program: is the overall initiative that exists to ensure the achievement of the strategic objectives and the benefits of a process strategy.

Project: is the tactical initiative that implements a single process, and other discreet pieces of well-defined work, such as procurement of a BPMS.

Process: is implemented by the project and is the repeatable operational result that runs thereafter.

For each of these stages there are Sponsors, Owners and Managers. These are roles, not jobs, held by managers in addition to their other roles. The roles may be held sequentially by the same people, for example a Program Sponsor may become a Program Owner, decide to be a Project Owner, then become Process Owner. The unshaded boxes in the table below detail who appoints the person in the role, or in the first row what the person does.

Role Stage	Program	Project	Process
Sponsor	Initiates the program	Is the Program Owner	-
Owner	Program Sponsor	Program Owner	Program Owner
Manager	Program Owner	Project Owner	Process Owner

All of these roles are cross-functional. It is important that those in these roles have the ability to put the enterprise's interests above those of the particular function for which they may be responsible. These are enterprise roles; in effect they are acting as part of the CEO's office.

Program roles

Program Sponsor

The word 'Sponsor' may be used in an organisation instead of 'Owner', and this is acceptable; however, there is a difference in meaning. A Sponsor is the person approached to support a new idea, or in this case a program, and so ensures that the program gets up and running. The Sponsor then passes the program to the Owner who is responsible through to its completion. For example, the CEO is responsible for the strategic plan or overall strategy of the organisation and will sponsor individual strategies and programs until they are assigned to individual executives who become the Owners. Of course, the Sponsor may become the Owner.

The Program Sponsor:

- Outlines the program needed to implement the strategy
- Identifies a BPM Consultant or Specialist who will bring expert knowledge to the program, and who will assist the program from as early as possible. This person has the experience to help the Sponsor in the next activity
- Builds the business case
- Obtains organisational approval for the program
- Identifies the Program Owner (may be him/herself)
- Passes responsibility to the Program Owner

Program Owner

A process program is the strategic initiative put in place to realise the business benefits of one or more business strategies. The program is owned by the executive responsible for the key strategy or the most senior executive if there is ambiguity about strategy ownership. It is unacceptable for the ownership of a program to be delegated to a mid-level manager as this sends a message that the program is not of critical importance to the organisation but is merely tactical.

The Program Owner:

- Demonstrates the organisation's commitment by endorsing and promoting the program—conveying it is essential to the long-term survival and growth of the organisation and its strategic alignment
- Ensures that the organisational environment is conducive to success
- Provides political and practical cover for the program and ensures that it is not derailed, while nurturing the program and ensuring its meaningful survival and success
- Ensures that the program continues to meet the strategic objectives of the organisation in an efficient and appropriate manner
- Funds the program budget or ensures funds are assigned
- Ensures the program secures the right senior people resources
- Selects the Program Manager and ensures his/her effectiveness
- Sponsors projects and selects Project Owners (or takes on the role) and ensures their effectiveness
- Ensures that the evolving processes support organisational policies, governance processes and legal and regulatory obligations
- Provides process tools, including information systems, which are used across many Process Projects and running processes
- Provides the Program Manager's and Project Owner's training or induction

- Measures business benefits delivered against those targeted by the strategy
- Chairs the BPM Strategy Group comprising the Program Owner and other senior executive stakeholders (depending upon the organisation)
- Oversees and coordinates project managers
- Ensures process projects are opened and closed as needed

The owner needs to not only demonstrate commitment, but also seek the contribution of all stakeholders so that the best result can be obtained with the minimum of friction. It is a political role and a person of reputation and influence is needed.

Program Manager

The Program Manager is the person responsible for the program and may be in the role full-time (it may be that there are no other full-time participants). The role is challenging and a very good vehicle for a fast-rising middle business manager as it has an enterprise perspective and develops influence skills.

The process of innovation requires intensive communication and it is up to the program manager to create an environment in which communication can flow easily and new ideas can flourish.

The Program Manager:

- Manages the program
- Agrees upon the scope of the program, in consultation with the project owner, BPM expert and stakeholders
- Agrees upon program terms of reference with the project owner

- Drafts and maintains the program timeline (exact date scheduling does not work well with programs)
- Allocates work to the program team and others
- Manages program communications and presentations
- Arranges program team meetings
- Advises the program owner as to
  ○ Project Portfolio inclusions and priorities
  ○ Project cost and resource estimates
  ○ Senior resource issues
  ○ Stakeholder issues
  ○ Alignment with strategic goals and objectives
- Liaises with stakeholders
- Reports on the program to the BPM Strategy Group

BPM specialist

The program needs someone with well-developed BPM (not BPMS) skills. This person will develop/provide the standard formats and templates used by all process projects and contribute skills and experience to the program and to the Program Owner.

The BPM Specialist may be the Program Manager.

This person(s) will probably be assigned to all projects and probe and push the project teams into examining alternative and better process ideas and delivering process innovation. Their role includes taking the workshop discussions and whiteboard outputs and converting them into diagrams and documents between workshops.

Communications specialist

Program and Project teams often write their own communications, this has issues: a) they may not relate to their audience; b) they may not be very good at it; c) they may not be aware of all of the communication channels available; d) they may not be able to 'brand' the eventual new process and system well, which is important in driving acceptance; e) they get so involved in the work that they fail to issue enough or timely communications; and f) they may not be able to write communications on behalf of the owner, who is often the person who needs to be identified with the communication.

For all these reasons it is best to have someone from the communications department assigned to the program who will develop and issue all communications.

Project management administrator

A person with project management experience supports the Program and Project Leaders by providing and maintaining whatever project management tools and templates are agreed upon at the program level. Given project involvement, this has the advantage that the person can maintain program information easily. Alternatively, the BPM Specialist may have the skills to undertake this role.

Process team members

Process program and project team members are mostly drawn from across the organisation—people who have everyday roles in the operation of the business and are not specialists in process work. It is essential to use business people from everyday roles so as to make sure the process designs are grounded in reality.

Experience shows that the best ideas for process innovation come from the building of ideas amongst the people who know most about the area of focus, and sometimes from the most unexpected quarter—never assume someone who holds back or does not participate at first is not going to contribute some flash of brilliance later.

Program cycle

A program can run over a number of years with many process projects. The process program can be part of a transformation program. A process program typically goes through the following cycle.

- Set up program
- Do program planning
- Manage program
- Complete process architecture top levels
- Prioritise and select processes
- Agree on technical strategy
- Develop processes (multiple streams)
    ◦ Design high–level process
    ◦ Initiate project
    ◦ Oversee project
    ◦ Close project
- Close program

These stages are discussed in detail below.

Set up program

Appoint Sponsor

The executive, having decided upon a process strategy in support of one or more corporate goals, appoint a sponsor for the program who will realise the strategy.

Appoint Stakeholder Management Group (SMG)

The Sponsor assembles a stakeholder management group (this may be done by the Program Owner). The members are executives and are at the same level as the Program Owner. Their role is to ensure that the strategy is being implemented and to manage the portfolio decisions. The Program Owner chairs this group.

This group will make the preliminary policy and resource decisions to set up the program and announces the program. One of the key decisions to be made by this group is how the program and projects will be resourced, are people going to work full-time or part-time?

The group will:

- Agree program principles and rules of engagement.
- Make strategic recommendations for the program.
- Manage the program portfolio. See Appendix A for an example of a portfolio management process.
- Prioritise projects and develop outline project timing so as to deliver an integrated BPM program that best uses the available monetary and human resources, in order to deliver best value to the organisation in support of the strategic plan. An example of a process outline for submission to the SMG for approval is shown in Appendix B.
- Maintain a portfolio list of potential process and information management projects; approve changes recommended by the Program Management Group (PMG), see below.
- Commission business cases or papers in support of potential projects.
- Review competing demands for scarce resources needed to staff and equip those projects.

- Recommend to the Program Owner which projects to initiate and which key resources to assign to these projects
- Support roadblock elimination, when sought by PMG

Agree terms of reference

The SMG reviews the strategy and materials and details the terms of reference for the program. The terms of reference are broad and provide a bridge from the business strategy to the program. The terms of reference may include:

- Corporate goals the program is intended to contribute towards achieving.
- Program approach, being the result of the SMG deliberations
- Intended business benefits
- Outline timeline targets
- SMG portfolio management procedures
- Program roles and responsibilities
- Recommendations to the Program Owner for PMG members

Appoint Program Owner

The Sponsor identifies a Program Owner or confirms his/her continuance in this role.

Identify and appoint BPM Specialist/Consultant

A BPM Specialist or Consultant is the key facilitator of the Process Program, this person brings the knowledge, experience, expertise and methods and tools used in the program. The knowledge is conveyed to all who participate in the program over time and the teams become increasingly confident and capable in their process work.

The BPM Specialist is identified and appointed by the Program Sponsor. The BPM Specialist joins both the SMG and PMG (see below) to provide continuity and consistency.

Appoint Program Manager

The Owner identifies and appoints a Program Manager. The Program Manager joins both the SMG and PMG (see next paragraph) to provide continuity and consistency.

Set up Program Management Group (PMG)

The Program Owner assembles a group of stakeholder managers together with the BPM Specialist and the Program Manager who will undertake program work in workshop and be responsible for the program day-to-day. The Program Owner may chair these meetings or hand the chair to the Program Manager.

The PMG will not only undertake program workshops but also oversee process projects later on. Its responsibilities include the following. Much of the documentation preparation and everyday program work will be done by the Program Manager and/or BPM Specialist.

- Provide BPM expertise.
- Manage the program.
- Identify process stakeholders.
- Determine program goals, principles, objectives and measures in support of the business strategy.
- Propose new projects and approve documentation, see Appendix C for example Project Terms of Reference inclusions.
- Approve Process Profiles; see Appendix D for a Process Profile format. Not all fields can be completed at this stage but it is

a valuable thinking tool for teasing out issues and objectives from all perspectives.

- Workshop high level designs in early stages of the program.
- Receive project reports and advise project leaders.
- Consider project resource changes.
- Review the need for any new BPMS or information management software and recommend initiation of asset acquisition or build projects.
- Assess choice of software and recommend authorisation of its acquisition to the Program Owner.
- Identify project business leaders, investigate their involvement and recommend their appointment to the Program Owner.
- Advise the Program Owner.

Assemble process program team

The Program Manager assembles a small program team. There will be a communications specialist but that person may just be assigned from the Communications Department on an 'as and when needed' basis. The team is usually small and comprises analysts and planners. The support people in the team not only support the program leaders but also perform Program Support Office (PSO) and Project Management Office (PMO) functions. PMO people may not be added until the first projects starts.

For smaller programs some of the management groups and roles may be merged.

Do program planning

The PMG debates the program goals, principles and objectives. Goals, principles and objectives reflect each other and the strategy the program is intended to realise. For example, if the strategy is to raise customer acquisition and retention by implementing better processes, one of the goals may be to have customers view the organisation as delivering the best value in the industry—then a principle may be to have process projects focus on customer value before cost objectives. In this case improving customer value is backed up by value measurements based on customers' input.

This sequence ensures that the intended business benefits, which are mentioned in the strategy and goal, are defined in the program at a level at which measures are feasible. There is a business planning technique 'Results Chain' also known as 'Benefits Realisation' that readers may use to assist them with this planning.

Programs may include related projects that are necessary to deliver a strategy, for example, training, job families, remuneration structures, incentives and other HR matters that will support the introduction of a new process.

Principles are not a conventional inclusion in management methodologies but their use provides decision making guidelines for the program and is valuable for process projects in determining the optimum process design. Here are some examples:

- Customer Service is paramount.
- Resource allocation should not be constrained by existing reporting lines.
- Current policy applies, any changes are to be referred to the SMG.
- Design and implement smart processes and systems that are easy to use, obviate unnecessary activities, ensure policy adherence, and improve the quality of the customer experience and staff working life.

- Improve efficiency and reduce the staff resource time consumed by processes, and/or reduce the need for additional staff as work load grows.
- Remove the disparate methods and tools currently in use in favour of consistent, single, more efficient organisation-wide processes and systems.
- Escalations should only occur after at least two reminders/ warnings.

Much of the program planning is undertaken by the program team, for example:

- List stakeholders
- Provide ball park estimates for financial planning, these are indicators, not firm estimates
- Undertake program planning, develop a program roadmap
- Schedule projects at the macro level to optimise the use of resources and integrate project planning for the whole program

A program is about sense-making and uncertainty, so planning should not be rigid and over-quantified. Scheduling is not like project scheduling which is more definitive and controlled, it is better to plan target dates rather than detailed task durations. This approach requires stakeholders to maintain confidence as they do not have a firm detailed schedule to gauge progress, which is what they are probably used to if they are involved in project management.

Manage program

Once the planning has been done, the Program Manager and his/ her team manage and support the program on a day-to-day basis, reporting to the Program Owner. The team undertakes these functions:

Act as Program Support Office (PSO)

- Recommend decision preferences to SMG and PMG.
- Provide strategy and policy advice in support of projects and the program.
- Schedule and resource PMG meetings.
- Collect project reports and measures and table at PMG meetings.
- Recommend portfolio changes.
- Maintain the program portfolio.
- Oversee delivery of projects in the program, including receiving summary status reports from project leaders in meetings.
- Assist Program Owner, Program Manager and BPM Specialist.

Not only does the team support the program, but because the program has oversight over projects, the team will provide project support—at least with regard to process knowledge. If there is no corporate project management office (PMO) then the team will fulfill that function as well and provide project management expertise and knowledge.

Act as Project Management Office (PMO).

- Review project terms of reference.
- Set up and maintain standard documentation, templates and methodology guidelines for projects.
- Set up project reporting and procedures.
- Provide assistance to project teams in overcoming obstacles.
- Build a knowledgebase of lessons learned.
- Provide project management support to project teams.

Similarly, the team may provide full communications support to the communications specialist or may merely provide communications content for a corporate communications office to develop and maintain, including website development and maintenance and provision of hot desk and other go-live support.

Provide communications services

- Set up and maintain websites
- Develop branding strategies
- Develop communications plans
- Draft and publish program communications
- Provide feedback gathering services
- Prepare go-live communications packages
- Provide 'hot desks' and other go-live support

Complete process architecture top levels

In addition to managing the program, some program operational activities are undertaken before projects can be initiated. These activities define high level process information, providing greater clarity for the oversight of individual projects.

Key business processes

The program kicks off in earnest with a workshop with the SMG run by the Program Manager and BPM Specialist to define the key business processes. These are refined by the program team and confirmed with the SMG as an agenda item at a later SMG meeting.

It is a great advantage to work on the key business processes with the SMG. An introduction at the workshop is used to provide updates on plans, and then the key business processes activity helps secure SMG commitment and awareness.

There are typically 6 to 12 key business processes. An example is:

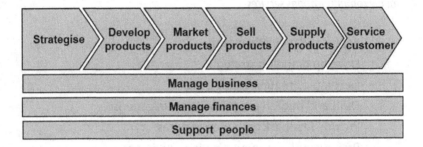

Conventionally, everything above the activity level (Key Processes, Processes and Subprocesses) are shown as broad arrows, excepting support processes which may be shown in boxes to distinguish them from primary processes. The boxes may be shown alongside or under the arrows spread across the full width in order to portray support.

This format bears a marked resemblance to the concept of Value Chains expounded by Michael Porter:

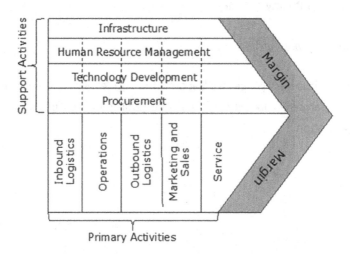

Porter was concerned with competitive advantage. 'The value chain is a systematic approach to examining the development of competitive advantage. The chain consists of a series of activities that create and build value. They culminate in the total value delivered by an organisation.'[xiv] This is exactly what we are saying about processes. So, the concept of Key Business Processes has parallels in other branches of management thinking, but we would use the word 'processes' instead of 'activities' used in the value chain.

As an example, a university senior management team might come up with the following key process diagram. In this example support processes are shown as boxes after the primary process arrows:

The key business process map may be revisited later in the program, if improvements become apparent, but it is important that the original team buy into any changes.

Commence process architecture

The key business processes become the top level of the enterprise process architecture, which covers everything that occurs within the organisation.

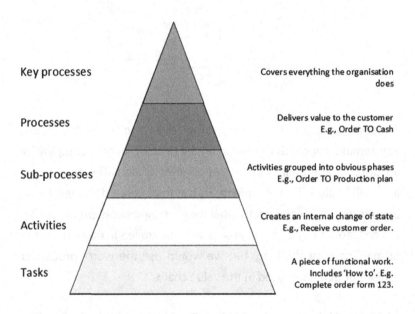

Key processes	Covers everything the organisation does
Processes	Delivers value to the customer E.g., Order TO Cash
Sub-processes	Activities grouped into obvious phases E.g., Order TO Production plan
Activities	Creates an internal change of state E.g., Receive customer order.
Tasks	A piece of functional work. Includes 'How to'. E.g. Complete order form 123.

Purpose of the architecture

- Developing a complete enterprise process architecture helps with the elimination of overlapping processes, and sub-processes can be normalised (only developed once). Individual processes may then be able to adopt existing subprocess modules and reduce work required on new processes. This aligns with the IT 'services' concept in systems design.

- Having a complete process architecture assists the prioritisation of processes. There is greater clarity, and discussion is facilitated between stakeholders when setting process priorities.

- A process architecture ensures that processes are not missed, the architecture is developed top-down making it easier to identify all processes.

- The process architecture becomes part of the detail supporting the business model.

- The Program Team maintains the process architecture as it is developed. This includes adding activity and task detail during process projects.

Process charts

The PMG, in workshop with the Program Manager and BPM Specialist, fills out the processes for selected key business processes, expanding the second level of the architecture.

The process chart for the university Enquiry TO Alumni key business process might look like:

Each arrow is a process that results in the delivery of value to the customer, in this example, the student. Arrow symbols are used to

indicate a key business process, a process or a sub-process, whereas activities are shown as boxes. The use of 'TO' in the process name enables the start and finish of the process to be defined and is another indication of a process.

This may be when the organisation begins to realise there are more processes operating in the organisation than was previously assumed, but they have never been named as such before. The rule is strictly applied that a process must be end-to-end and produce measurable value.

Process deconstruction diagram

A process deconstruction diagram covers two levels of the process architecture. The diagram drawn here relates processes to their key business processes. The example shown is for a university.

The second level 'Enquiry TO Alumni' above appears as column 3 on the diagram.

Note that a numbering system has been added, each level adds '-xx' to the code for the level above.

The diagram is a valuable communication device. It can be shown to the SMG to illustrate on a single slide the number of processes in the organisation. It can also be used to show progress, and to discuss the next stage, which is the selection of priority processes.

All of the above work is diagramming processes as they are today, called the 'AS IS' state. Too little information is available to work on the future state, called the 'TO BE' state, and although there is a strong temptation to dive into the 'TO BE' design, resist it until the AS IS has been completed. Eventually, the diagram may be amended to show 'TO BE' process designs, but that is much later.

University Deconstruction Diagram

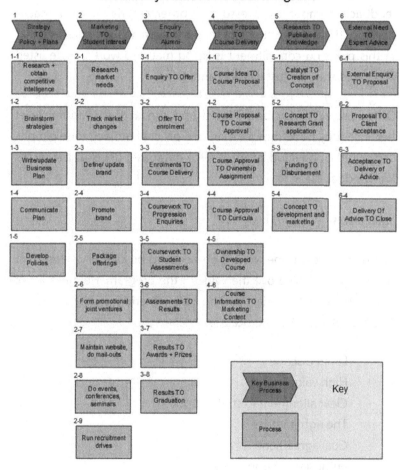

1
Strategy TO Policy + Plans

2
Marketing TO Student Interest

3
Enquiry TO Alumni

4
Course Proposal TO Course Delivery

5
Research TO Published Knowledge

6
External Need TO Expert Advice

1-1 Research + obtain competitive intelligence	**2-1** Research market needs	**3-1** Enquiry TO Offer	**4-1** Course Idea TO Course Proposal	**5-1** Catalyst TO Creation of Concept	**6-1** External Enquiry TO Proposal
1-2 Brainstorm strategies	**2-2** Track market changes	**3-2** Offer TO enrolment	**4-2** Course Proposal TO Course Approval	**5-2** Concept TO Research Grant application	**6-2** Proposal TO Client Acceptance
1-3 Write/update Business Plan	**2-3** Define/ update brand	**3-3** Enrolments TO Course Delivery	**4-3** Course Approval TO Ownership Assignment	**5-3** Funding TO Disbursement	**6-3** Acceptance TO Delivery of Advice
1-4 Communicate Plan	**2-4** Promote brand	**3-4** Coursework TO Progression Enquiries	**4-4** Course Approval TO Curricula	**5-4** Concept TO development and marketing	**6-4** Delivery Of Advice TO Close
1-5 Develop Policies	**2-5** Package offerings	**3-5** Coursework TO Student Assessments	**4-5** Ownership TO Developed Course		
	2-6 Form promotional joint ventures	**3-6** Assessments TO Results	**4-6** Course Information TO Marketing Content		
	2-7 Maintain website, do mail-outs	**3-7** Results TO Awards + Prizes			
	2-8 Do events, conferences, seminars	**3-8** Results TO Graduation			
	2-9 Run recruitment drives				

Key Business Process

Key

Process

Prioritise and select processes

Prioritise processes

The team agrees process priorities by referring to areas of 'pain', strategic imperative, synergy with other strategic programs, customer feedback, competitive pressure or other criteria. The list that is developed is the starting point for portfolio management. Note that at this point no commitment is being made to work on the listed processes, they are just project candidates.

Other projects may be initiated and run at the program level because they benefit more than one process project, for example: select BPMS; develop process roles database; develop processes knowledgebase.

Select process

The first process to be worked on needs to be carefully selected, it must succeed and prove the value of the program. Here is a list of seven suggested criteria[xv] but the 'pain' criterion usually surfaces a short list of top priority processes:

- Limited scope
- High value
- Clear alignment to strategic goals
- The right metrics
- Goal agreement
- Enthusiastic business sponsor
- Business user engagement

Each process will have at least one project. If it is decided that a large or complicated process is to be completed in phases then there may be a succession of linked projects and team membership may change between projects.

Once the first project is under way the next and successive processes are selected from the portfolio. It may be decided for risk management reasons that the first process completion be awaited before proceeding with the next process, but after that multiple processes may be worked on in parallel.

Typically, the portfolio will be divided into different stages for projects, for example: identified; business case requested; approved and pending; initiated; progressing; operational/closed.

Ownership

The Program Owner may decide to take on the role of Project Owner or appoint a senior person who will obtain business benefit from the process outcomes but does not have the time to be the Project Leader. The PMG may recommend a Project Owner to the Program Owner.

This step may be left until the process project is initiated as the Program Owner is the Project Sponsor and will own project initiation.

Stakeholders

The PMG should list the stakeholders in the process. This is to ensure that they, or their representatives, are candidates for project team selection and so that they will in due course be invited to stakeholder sessions. The PMG should ensure the wider or system view is taken by considering all who may be impacted by changing the process.

Scope

It is not unusual to find that a process that has been identified and nominated into the portfolio is in fact only part of the process. This is because people are in the habit of thinking at the functional or subprocess level. The questions, 'Is there customer value produced at the end of the process?' and 'Are there earlier activities occurring in the organisation that contribute to the customer value and should therefore be included in the process?' should be asked to ensure the full process is being included in the scope.

Agree technical strategy to support business strategy and program

A technical strategy which supports the business strategy and the program is a critical success factor. Whilst the technical strategy and technical architecture is a matter for the Chief Technical Officer (CTO) and IT department, it is important to make clear the business preferences for the type of tool that will best support the organisation's processes. There are a number of considerations to be taken into account when determining the technical strategy.

Technical platform

The technical platform that best supports a process business strategy and program is some form of workflow management platform which will accept many different processes.

Most organisations will already have some high volume transaction processes managed by enterprise systems such as enterprise resource planning (ERP), customer relationship management (CRM), Finance and HR systems and possibly industry-specific operational systems or even dedicated custom-built systems.

If the organisation has industry-specific or dedicated operational systems the process program is about lower volume processes with high user populations (low volume, low user population processes may not cost justify themselves). These sorts of processes, in fact, constitute the largest number of processes in a service organisation.

If the organisation does not have enough industry-specific or dedicated operational systems then some high-volume, high-user-population processes will also be included in the process program.

The other system factor to consider is level of automation (meaning an activity is completed by the computer system without any human involvement) versus computerisation (meaning human input of information for each activity). Many administrative systems have low levels of automation even though they are computerised.

Even low-volume, low-user-number, low-automation processes will benefit from process innovation. And such processes may be computerised using everyday 'desktop' or low cost enterprise systems. Even a defined workflow using email and attached forms can be a real improvement over manual systems.

Organisations often have forms on their websites; however, this does not necessarily mean there is a workflow system behind the forms. They may just be printed out for a manual process or entered into a database system. So, if a process is said to be computerised make sure there is a workflow system that receives the form and routes it to successive people who complete the necessary activities to finish the process.

The following table suggests different types of technical platforms for different process criteria. Nevertheless, every organisation will need to evaluate its own best solution.

Number of transactions	Number of users	Proportion of automated activities	Type of platform
High	High	High/Medium	Industry system, dedicated system
Medium	High	Medium/Low	Enterprise system (ERP, CRM, etc.)
High/ Medium/Low	High/Medium	Medium/Low	Fully featured BPMS suite
Medium/Low	Medium	Low	Simple workflow/ low cost BPMS
Medium/Low	Medium/Low	Low	Desktop tools, e.g., email, PC-database systems, simple web systems

Whilst it may be feasible to use an existing enterprise system that has workflow capabilities it is usually better to set up a BPMS which has been developed to manage multiple workflows.

Integration

A good technical strategy should provide a means of ensuring data is only held once (referred to as 'normalising' the data) otherwise differences creep in as data is updated and errors result. A BPMS can be used to define processes that call on data from, and save data to, existing databases, so that data is normalised across the enterprise, thereby integrating the BPMS with existing systems. Most BPMS provide interface modules for the most common enterprise systems to facilitate integration.

However, integration does bring complexities and can hold up the implementation of processes on the BPMS. Other systems may need to be modified due to the implementation of the new process. There is an interim strategy whereby processes use a new local database, which is synchronised with other databases manually or by running a script. This enables a new process to be set up and run whilst not adding the complication of integration. When the process is running satisfactorily the integration can be undertaken. This approach is recommended so that processes can be implemented in a reasonable time period, rather than waiting for full integration.

A big advantage of adding a BPMS in an organisation with heavy investment in old database systems is that it enables a modern user interface to be added whilst retaining the existing investment in databases.

Roles database

Processes have roles defined to fit the particular needs of the process. Process role names may not match job titles. The process needs to know who has a job role so that it can address emails to the correct person. It may need to know who is an alternate for that person if they do not complete a task on time, or for when a person is away, and in the latter case it will need to know effective planned dates when there is a switch.

A relational database is needed that holds all this information. This may be part of the BPMS or it may be necessary to set up a roles database external to the BPMS.

This database will hold valuable organisational data, so before long, people may try and use the roles database for other activities for which a process has not yet been configured. If the database is separate then small 'utilities' can be written to support other work, but it is better if the databases are not directly manipulated as this can cause errors in process data.

Technical platform acquisition

Once the technical strategy is defined, the program can set terms of reference for a project to acquire and configure the technical platform, including the application, to be used for all processes within the program and initiate the project.

Develop process (multiple streams)

Design high level process

DESIGN AT PROGRAM OR PROJECT LEVEL?

High-level process designs may be completed before a project is initiated as this is a good way of increasing certainty for the project phase. The high-level designs include the AS IS, the TO BE, and if done separately, the SYSTEM designs. 'High-level' may mean at subprocess or activity level. How process designs are developed is explained in later chapters.

These high-level designs together take much less time to complete than working out the detailed designs at the procedural or business requirements level. The high-level designs become terms of reference for the process project(s).

If the high-level designs are done at the program level the PMG defines the designs, drafting in people who do the work as needed. But *it is essential that these people be involved*, leaving process design to managerial and professional people alone will not result in the best solution.

Doing the high-level designs at the program level encourages free thinking and innovation, but it will often need attendance by people who may later be project team members. As a result, there may be debate about whether high-level designs should be done within the project, rather than at program level. This really depends on the quality of the project leader. If the project leader is a strategic thinker and is intent upon transforming his/her area and is the true primary beneficiary of the process then it can make sense to let the project team define the high-level design under the leadership of the project leader. If the leader uses a project manager or IT manager style—focusing on output at the possible expense of radical thinking—rather than an open business leader style then high-levels designs should definitely be done at the program level.

If the high-level design is done at program level the BPM specialist or consultant will, in any case, present the design to the project team at the first project meeting and there is opportunity then to see whether there are some improvements to be made.

There is an intermediate strategy whereby the project is initiated, the AS IS is completed, and the program team and project team, or a subgroup, work on the TO BE and SYSTEM designs together. Following that, the project team completes the business requirements.

The approach to be used needs to be agreed at the SMG level with PMG input. The decision may be varied by project as it depends upon the style of the selected leader.

PHASING PROCESSES

Some processes are quite long because they are end-to-end, for example, one of the commonest and longest processes used in any organisation is 'Order TO Cash', which encompasses a large part of what the organisation does operationally. In the interests of creating short projects, processes may be broken into a number of subprocesses after a high–level process design has been developed, and each subprocess will have a project initiated for its detailed design. Note that the subprocesses are not by function, they are by process phase, for example, for the Order TO Cash process: 'Order TO Plan', Plan TO Delivery', 'Delivery TO Payment' may be the subprocesses.

PROCESS NAME FORMAT

The format for the name 'Xxx TO Yxx' used above is the formal way of naming a process or subprocess, its advantage is that it clearly defines scope. The name will be abbreviated and the rule then is to put a verb first, to denote activity, for example 'Plan order', 'Deliver order' and 'Obtain payment'.

Initiate project

The program maintains the portfolio and when a process is selected and approved the program team initiates individual process projects.

Project terms of reference

The BPM Specialist and Program Manager write terms of reference for the first project. If high level designs have been completed they will be appended. See Appendix C for a Project Terms of Reference format.

Appoint Project Leader

The Owner identifies and arranges the Project Leader's appointment for the first project. At this point the program passes accountability to the project leader. Several process projects may be run in parallel, but staggered, the program team determines how this will occur.

Appoint project team members

The Owner and the Leader select and appoint the core project team.

Oversee project

Project Leaders report to the Program Owner regularly. The Program Manager arranges the PMG/Program Team meetings at which the Project Leaders report on their projects' progress and issues and other program matters are discussed.

The PMG does not participate in the projects, although individual members may take on a role in a project.

The PMG provides the project interface with the program and its strategy. The PMG's responsibility is to ensure that the project is set up to succeed and receives the necessary support to succeed.

Close project

Once a process goes live, the program team must ensure that the project closes in good time and the project team is disbanded. Sometime well after processes go live the Program Manager convenes a post–implementation review meeting. All members of the project team, the PMG and Program Team, and the post project Process Owner and Manager are invited. The purpose of the meeting is to identify lessons learned that can be used to improve the program and project methodologies.

Close program

The SMG closes the program because all approved projects have been completed or because of a change in strategy.

CHAPTER **3**

Managing Projects — Planning and Delivering the Change

Project organisation

Each process project has its own team. This way multiple projects can be run in parallel within one program. Some project roles may be undertaken by people with program roles, but in the main, the people are different—bringing specialist knowledge and expertise for the particular process on which the project works.

Project management is a well-established discipline well documented elsewhere, so we will only go into detail with respect to what is particularly relevant and in some cases a little different for process projects.

Firstly, the project roles.

Project roles

Project Owner:

Ensures the project supports the process strategy and program:

- Ensures project terms of reference and project progress support the current organisation policy
- Owns project, supports it, nurtures it, provides an organisational 'umbrella'
- Funds or identifies the budget
- Monitors realisation of the business benefits of the project
- Selects the Project Leader, arranges training and ensures effectiveness
- Provides project tools, including information systems
- Measures project effectiveness
- Liaises with the Program Owner and operational leaders to select and appoint the Process Owner before project completion
- Assists the Process Owner in selecting and appointing the Process Manager before project completion
- Determines project closure and ensures post-implementation review occurs
- Passes responsibility for implemented process to Process Owner
- Is a member of the SMG

Notes:

a) The Project Sponsor role is undertaken by the Program Owner, being the person who initiates the new project.
b) The Program Owner will often choose to act as Project Owner, depending upon the number of projects run in parallel. The

reason for this is so that the project objectives and business benefits are always to the fore as the project progresses. The Owner does not need to attend all project meetings, so the time required is not excessive.

c) This, therefore, may result in the three roles of Program Owner, Project Sponsor and Project Owner being undertaken by one person, this simplifies communications and is perfectly acceptable practice.

Project Leader

Directs and coordinates the project, manages the following:

- Agreement on the scope of the project, in consultation with the project owner, BPM specialist or consultant and stakeholders
- Agreement on project terms of reference with the project owner
- Determination, monitoring, and review of staffing requirements for the project team
- Review and amendment or development of the AS IS, TO BE and SYSTEM high-level process designs and process profile, and any other selected templates
- Setting of target dates and work plans
- Allocation of work to the project team and others
- Chairing of project team meetings
- Lead development of business requirements including workflows
- Review and finalisation of the following drafts to be used in system development
  ◦ workflows and activity definitions
  ◦ screen mock-ups

- ○ business rules
- ○ procedural help pop-up screens and website notes
- ○ emails, report formats and other business documentation
- Development of workflow, information and reporting systems, including user interfaces
- Project communications and presentations, the 'sell' of the new process and system
- Provision of business and user perspectives, representation of organisational interests, consultation with other business managers to ensure process and system value to users and the organisation
- Advising the project owner as to:
  - ○ Marginal costs
  - ○ Resource issues
  - ○ Project timing and target dates
  - ○ Significant stakeholder issues
  - ○ Alignment with strategic goals and objectives
- 'Fronting' the project team to stakeholders and liaison with stakeholders as to process and system common interests and stakeholder requests
- Reporting on the project to the PMG
- Review and finalisation of the process and system
- Process and system test and pilot before go-live
- Go-live
- Preparation of incoming Process Manager for transition from implementation to business operating stage, hand over, close project
- Initial support to Process Manager and drafting responses to user queries for issue by the process Manager

Note:

a) The Project Leader, who ideally is the primary business beneficiary of the new process, may become the Process Owner or Manager after the process is implemented.

Project team members

Team members will be operational managers and front-line people who have the best knowledge of the process. Team membership may vary over time as people with knowledge of particular subprocesses or activities are brought in to contribute their knowledge and ideas.

Pick the right people who will contribute, this is about people's character rather than their job roles. It is as much about potential as it is about their known skills.

It is necessary to establish whether the right people are available; and if they are wanted full-time, what it would take to extricate them from their current roles. The best people are always busy so work-arounds will often be necessary. This is where an effective Owner can contribute political skills and influence.

One quandary is what to do about political appointees, that is, people being volunteered to just watch and report back and if necessary put up barriers on behalf of an antagonistic stakeholder functional manager. The question to ask is whether the person is good in his/her own right. If so, then you need to believe in the rightness of the process and project to convince the person that they should contribute and to advise their manager that the project is beneficial. The 'turning' of the person should not be deceitful, the project should speak for itself.

In terms of team size, keep it small, 4 to 8 is ideal, 10 to 12 is manageable, but more than that should be avoided. The team must be small enough to avoid formation of internal factions that take up different positions, it is important that the team remain cohesive and can work out its differences.

BPM and Communications Specialists

Refer to Program Roles above, the specialists will most likely wear both program and project hats.

Project phases

The following is a summary of the project phases. Each phase will be examined in greater detail later on.

Prepare the process project

A project is initiated and resourced by the program. It is essential that project terms of reference are clear and unambiguous if the project is to succeed; it is the responsibility of the program team to create certainty before the project is launched. The terms of reference for the project are signed off by the Program Owner. The Project Leader convenes the team and reviews the Project Terms of Reference and The Process Profile and then begins design.

Develop process

The development of the process has four steps:

The first three steps are all undertaken at the activity level, while the business requirements are developed at the procedural or task level. The first three steps do not take a great deal of time, two to three workshops are needed for each step. However, the business requirements take a lot longer because of the detail required and will take more time than for the other three steps put together.

The TO BE and SYSTEM designs may be merged into a single TO BE design if enough knowledge has been acquired about the BPMS and its capabilities, so that the TO BE is directly designed to take advantage of the BPMS technology.

The project team reviews the results of the first three steps together with other process materials, such as the Process Profile, and starts on the Business Requirements.

Specifying Business Requirements requires exact detail at the procedural level in workflow form, with all explanatory descriptions, context-sensitive help and other notes. The business requirements are best developed in collaboration with IT people as team members. The procedural information can then be immediately converted into 'screen paints' which can be refined iteratively. The IT developers then use the screen paints and detailed workflow to configure the BPMS for the process and editing continues iteratively.

More detail for each of the steps is provided later in the book.

Build system

The business requirements are frozen and the BPMS is configured for the process.

One of the key technical issues is integration with other systems and databases and this is examined in some detail later from a business information perspective.

A prototype system is shown to stakeholders as early as possible to get feedback and buy-in. The prototype is debugged and improved until a version is ready to be piloted.

System and user testing is essential before the system is ready for implementation.

Implement process and system

Pilot

No new process and system should ever go live without first having a pilot. A pilot is the running of the real system in a limited area of the organisation.

People expect new systems to run faultlessly or they quickly become disillusioned. However everyone knows that a pilot is run to find bugs and errors, so there is a much more accepting attitude and a real attempt to find errors. Errors may be process errors or configuration errors.

Enough time for effective piloting and rectification must be allowed before go live.

Implementation Planning

A tight and detailed project schedule is needed for an effective implementation.

ROLLOUT STRATEGY AND DETAILS

The rollout strategy will vary according to the number of stakeholders impacted by the new system. If the number of staff impacted is large then the project team will need to educate front-line managers and supervisors and provide them with materials so they can meet with their people all at the same time. This avoids rumours running ahead of the rollout. If the number is small, the Project team may educate stakeholders all together or at their own regular meetings, depending upon complexity.

PROCESS ROLE APPOINTMENTS

The Process Owner and Process Manager need to be appointed no later than at this time. They will take over responsibility for the process and the system when it goes live. In this way users will immediately refer issues to them rather than chasing project people after the project has closed.

TRAINING

These days training for a new system is done online. There may be merit in bringing users to a central training room with many computers, but this approach is more likely to be used during testing. Users need a 'sandpit' to try out the system, that is, a version of the system containing dummy data that users can experiment with and find their way through the process.

71

Users notoriously do not read manuals so the system should be as intuitive as possible and provide online context-sensitive help against each step in the process. High level notes about the process and policies can be provided on a web page from which the process is launched.

COMMUNICATIONS

The more people know what to expect, the better—use emails, websites and social media to tell stakeholders what is coming. It is important to let people know how they will be able to provide feedback. Easy feedback channels will help people deal with issues as they arise, so that they do not become irritated and start spreading a bad story.

TECHNICAL ENVIRONMENT SETUP

The IT people will need to complete infrastructure and database changes in readiness for go live.

HOT DESK AND FEEDBACK SETUP

Set up for phone, email and social media feedback. Make sure staff know they will be responsible for receiving the feedback, logging it and updating those who have provided it.

Go-live

On the go-live day the system is turned on, users start to use the process and system for real right across the organisation.

Acknowledge all feedback and indicate when the matter will be attended to. Keep a log of these promises and keep the person who provided the feedback up to date.

Close project

Within a week or two of go-live the project should be closed. The project must not be allowed to continue endlessly, with improvements being added progressively.

A suggested improvements list will have been started after completion of business requirements and will be steadily added to as people use the system and think of new ideas. The improvements log should be examined periodically by the program team to see whether a new project should be added to the portfolio. In any event, the Process Owner may ask for this.

Preparing the process project

Preparing for any project is essential to ensure its success. Diving in without adequate forethought and preparation increases the risk of failure and can in fact extend the project duration due to rework later on as misdirection or lack of buy-in is uncovered.

Project preparation will typically be undertaken by the program team and the outputs form part of the terms of reference for the project.

As the organisation becomes more experienced project preparation may be done by the appointed project leader and BPM specialist and approved by the program manager and owner.

The 'Prepare for Process' phase is illustrated in the following workflow diagram. The numbers in circles are connectors to the same numbers on later diagrams. Each activity is expanded upon below.

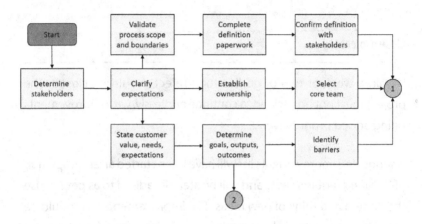

Determine stakeholders

In order to manage change effectively it is vital to identify all stakeholders. This requires probing and dialogue to ensure all stakeholders are identified. Here are some examples of stakeholders:

- Owners
- Managers
- Beneficiaries
- Contributors
- Advisers
- Performers
- Competitors (for resource, influence, control)
- CUSTOMER
- Customer interface (account management, sales, helpdesk, etc.)
- Marketing
- Others?

Clarify expectations

Understand what each stakeholder is expecting and why, do not assume common expectations. Some expectations may be hidden, probe to surface them; at the same time note any barriers for later. This is important because change is about people and we need to understand stakeholders' expectations in order to deal with politics. Politics is how people behave in an organisation, they are inevitable and must be accepted and worked with.

This stage of the program is about having conversations and meetings with knowledgeable people in order to gain their insight and to understand their assumptions. From these discussions a set of primary expectations is developed.

Once these have been developed they are presented back to the stakeholders and agreed during a meeting to confirm the project definition.

State customer value

The customer's viewpoint is not the same as an internal viewpoint. What value does the customer derive from the process? How does it help the customer deliver their product/service? A customer is only interested in what the service can do for his/her business, the value is about the customer's business, not the organisation's.

People who provide a service will typically over engineer a product or service, it is a matter of professional pride. If the customer's need is understood however, then unnecessary and costly work may be identified as unnecessary as it adds no customer value and can be eliminated.

A key consideration is the customer's assessment of time vs quality and cost—would the customer prefer a lower quality product delivered quickly or a higher quality product which takes longer and which is more expensive? Test this with the customer; the organisation's assumption is often wrong.

Another consideration is whether the organisation can delight its customer at no extra cost. This possibility is often surfaced once the customer value in really understood. To delight the customer is to retain the customer and provide a reference for prospects.

Validate scope and scope boundaries

Scope is easier to set if the process architecture has been worked out and the process can be seen in its architectural context.

Scope should not be restricted by organisational boundaries. Sometimes functional managers attempt to limit scope to conform to their territory so they can control the project—it is essential that such constraints be avoided otherwise you will no longer be working on an end-to-end process but on a subprocess. Even subprocesses should be defined by stages or phases of the process rather than functional boundaries; however, sometimes the two coincide.

The validation of scope is about getting buy-in from all of the key stakeholders. So, if a functional manager is powerful and tries to limit the scope then the other stakeholder managers need to be mobilised to provide an effective counter-balance, this will involve the sponsor and/or program manager.

For management and support processes there must be an organisational value produced (that is not just a functional or political value).

Determine goals, outputs, outcomes

Find out in broad business terms what the goals (as opposed to expectations) are for this process.

What are we trying to achieve? What outcomes are we after? What are the outputs or deliverables of the process? It is important to arrive at a broad view in answering these questions. Again, different stakeholders may have different perspectives and all of these perspectives need to be covered.

Value diagram

To reconcile the different perspectives of functions in the organisation it is best to assemble a stakeholder workshop and encourage the stakeholders to understand each other's perspective on value.

The Value Diagram is a simple thinking tool used to generate a multi-perspective value conversation amongst stakeholders. The version shown here represents the perspectives of Delivery, Business Unit, Marketing and Customer represented by Sales and/or Customer Accounts. The diagram can be adapted to the organisational spread of the particular process under discussion. The Goal is not shown on the diagram, this is agreed after the diagram is complete and participants can see the full spectrum of perspectives. The key achievement is moving thinking from outputs—which organisations focus on day-to-day—to outcomes, and from there to goals. As a thinking tool it is more about the discussion than the result.

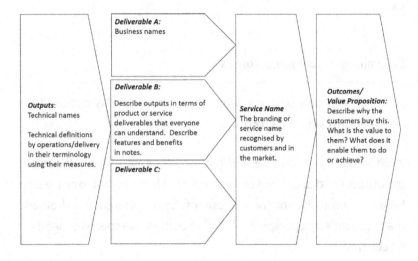

Outputs:
Technical names

Technical definitions
by operations/delivery
in their terminology
using their measures.

Deliverable A:
Business names

Deliverable B:
Describe outputs in terms of
product or service
deliverables that everyone
can understand. Describe
features and benefits
in notes.

Deliverable C:

Service Name
The branding or
service name
recognised by
customers and in
the market.

Outcomes/
Value Proposition:
Describe why the
customers buy this.
What is the value to
them? What does it
enable them to do
or achieve?

Identify barriers

It is a change management principle to identify and address barriers early. If they are left they gain strength and adherents. Be open to criticism during this phase, this is how you will identify barriers. Work out what is behind the criticism and how the criticism will be manifested in behaviours and objections: Who will front up? What justification will they present?

We will look at dealing with barriers in more detail in the change management chapter, but be aware that identifying and dealing with barriers needs to be done early on, before the project progresses into detail.

Establish ownership

There may not already be a Process Owner if the process is fractured into functional subprocesses, but initial process ownership is needed. Until the process is assembled and redesigned it may not be clear who the Process Owner should be. So, in practice what is likely to happen is that the Program Owner will act as Process Owner until the process project is well advanced.

Select core team

See earlier for the project team roles. By now the discussions with stakeholders will have clarified which functions need to be represented on the team and which business manager is the most likely candidate for the Project Leader role. The Project Owner needs to secure the commitment of these people and their managers for their inclusion in the team. Once all the team members have been identified and have committed then the BPM Specialist or Consultant briefs the new Project Leader as to how to precede with the project and the Leader calls the first team meeting.

Complete definition paperwork

Every organisation has its formal approval documents which need to be completed prior to stakeholder approval and sign off.

Confirm definition with stakeholders

After paper work is completed, the broad scope, goals and objectives are formally agreed with the management group and/or with stakeholders. It is important this occurs so that there is commitment at executive levels and amongst stakeholders. This avoids strategic issues being raised later as a basis for trying to close down the program because someone feels threatened as events unfold.

Once the project is prepared the next phase is mapping the AS IS.

CHAPTER 4

Mapping the AS IS — Gaining Insight

The AS IS is a description of how things are done at the commencement of the project. It may well not be recognised as a process, merely being seen as activities or tasks which have to be completed but with no formal links. Often the AS IS is not documented, people just know what they have to do, but in a fragmented way. Sometimes a system is seen as a process, but because historically many systems are function-specific, the system is actually for a subprocess and care must be taken to define the process scope as end-to-end.

Why not go straight to a new process?

Some will say mapping the AS IS is a waste of time—might as well get on with designing the new process. This is a mistake, it is important to have enough insight to make sure the new process is adequately defined, otherwise it is likely to miss things out and not cater for all the necessary variations. As a result, the new process will be criticised and/or abandoned.

Process vs procedure

These words are sometimes used synonymously but they have different meanings. A process describes the sequence of business activities that are undertaken from the beginning to the end in order to deliver a result of value for the customer—with the emphasis on activity, or what takes place. Whereas, a procedure describes how work is done in detail and fits the process directly into the organisation in terms of how the work is done and who does it.

A process may define which organisational unit is responsible for an activity but a procedure names the title or role of the person responsible. A procedure will detail technical requirements of a task, a process will not.

The procedural information is part of the business requirements for the system, and this ties the system to the process.

It is therefore important that business requirements be written by business people in the project team. The Project Leader has the most to gain by getting them right. A Business Analyst can assist with flowcharting and ensuring technical parameters are specified.

Levels of analysis

Many organisations make the mistake of analysing the AS IS at too low a level, the task level. This is not necessary and takes up a lot of time. In fact, it is better not to analyse the AS IS and TO BE at a low level as the chances of process innovation are greatly reduced because people cannot see the wood for the trees. People become absorbed with the fine detail of task work at this level and tend to be defensive about how they do their own work. This leads to entrenched positions and difficulty reaching agreement about changes. The result can be a patchwork of existing practices with some improvements. However, if teams are focused on the activity level the focus is not on *how* the work is done, but on *what* needs doing and *when* it is best done. This encourages innovative thinking.

Some organisations commission a dedicated process mapping team that maps AS IS processes before separate design teams works on the TO BEs. This is not recommended as it tends to lead to a task level AS IS definition which is distracting to TO BE teams and an unnecessary expense.

What is acceptable is to add notes about task information to activity boxes as the activity flow is developed, this enables people to express their concerns and for the team to gain insight whilst not allowing the task detail to overwhelm people's focus on activities

The AS IS process

The activities for mapping the AS IS are:

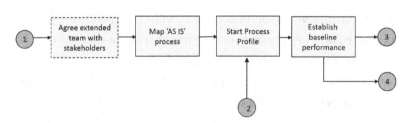

Dotted lines are used to denote that the activity is optional.

Agree AS IS team with stakeholders

This step is optional. There may be a difference between the team that maps the AS IS and that which designs the TO BE. A larger team including people who work on the process may be used to map the AS IS to ensure all activities are documented.

A stakeholder meeting compiles a list of all people doing work that appears to be part of the process and agrees to release these people to the AS IS workshops.

Map the AS IS

Process discovery starts with collecting all relevant documentation and accessing systems that may already provide some of the workflow functionality, or may be superseded by the new process and system.

Then an AS IS workshop is conducted with the team to map out how work is currently done. Progressively drawing the map on a whiteboard as people in the team explain what they do is the simplest mapping method.

Follow-up interviews or phone calls with stakeholders may be conducted one-on-one by two team members if some of the details are uncertain. These interviews are to clarify current practices; do not discuss any future process ideas, it is too early and will raise expectations that may be a distraction or may not be met.

The AS IS workflow is documented in a workflow mapping tool such as Visio (tools and templates are covered in the next section) and distributed for team members to review before the next workshop, when the process map is corrected.

Start process profile

Having completed the AS IS, the Profile is worked on to promote discussion of the key issues and objectives of the process, so that there is clarity going into the TO BE about what needs to be achieved. Not all of the Profile can be completed at this stage but information can be entered into most fields. The content can be updated again when the TO BE has been completed.

Establish baseline performance

Determine Process Measures

It is really important to measure the process you are working on, both before and after redesign—only then will you be able to establish what benefits have been realised. Here are some examples of process measures:[xvi]

- Cycle time
- Work (resource consumption) time and cost
- Customer satisfaction
- Staff satisfaction
- Management satisfaction
- Quantity of transactions per (time period)
- Transactions capacity per (time period)
- Error, complaint or rework volumes or costs
- Competitive score
- Quantity of process handoffs between different teams or departments
- Industry specific measures

Of these, the first two can be used on any process and should be the minimum measures taken.

Assess baseline performance

Once the measures have been agreed, the team must establish baseline performance for the process as it is before redesign commences. This may be difficult and exact measurement may not be possible, if so, assessments should be made. For cycle time, the minimum, average and maximum are probably needed. Do not be tempted to jump this step.

AS IS tools, templates and techniques

Most people can understand a flowchart and can sketch one out, the principles are easy to understand and the meaning is self-explanatory. Any process can be described in simple terms in this way.

There are some very clever software tools in the market and some people may delight in demonstrating their prowess in using these tools. My recommendation to you is not to be tantalised by such tools during the process design phase, there is plenty of time to use them later in the IT system design phase, after the key process innovations have been identified.

The tools that a process team uses should not get in the way of communication; it is the communication that generates innovation and good design. Accordingly, what follow in this chapter are unabashedly simple and commonplace tools that any business person can understand without difficulty—that *is* by design. Business users only work on process projects occasionally, they do not have the continual tool usage that a business analyst will have; and so, extended symbol sets used by advanced tools just get in the way. Sophisticated IT tools can be used later during the system development phase, when they are more suited to the task.

What follows details various tools, templates and techniques used during the AS IS phase. Further tools and techniques will be suggested for use in later stages, but many of the AS IS tools and techniques, particularly flow charts and workshops, are also used in later stages.

Workflow diagrams

Process flow diagrams, or flow charts, are the universal tool of BPM. A flow chart basically comprises boxes and arrows, each box being an activity and each arrow providing the flow information. Here is a simplified example of University Enquiry TO Offer.

One of the problems you will encounter is the question of whether you are working on a subprocess or an activity. An activity results in a change of state or an interim output. In the above example 'Approve application' may go to a number of people but the change of state does not occur until the application is approved, and you have an interim output which is an approved application. An activity does not define *how*. The steps which define how an application is approved are tasks.

Note the connection with the next process 'Student Offer TO Enrolment' at the end of the flow chart. This connection is optional.

Software flowchart tools

You can use a software tool such as Visio—as I have in the examples above—or any other of the many flowcharting software tools, for documenting flowcharts after the first workshop. In later workshops the software created flowcharts are projected on a screen and directly manipulated for changes. Others may use the charting tool on screen in the first and subsequent workshops without ever using the whiteboard; the danger is that participants get too wrapped up in watching how the tool works in that critical first workshop rather than thinking about the process.

Those who love IT tools may ask, why are you not using a BPMN (Business Process Management Notation) tool? We will look at BPMN tools when we come to Business Requirements, which is when they can be a fair choice, but they are better suited to be used at the task level, otherwise you may be dragged from the activity level down to the task level.

Role information

A lot of additional information can be added to a flowchart but be wary of overcomplicating it. One of the questions that arise is whether to add role information. In principle, it is better to not let the *Who* cloud the process, because later when the process is redesigned, activities may be reassigned. If responsibility has already been documented it tends to close down people's consideration of revised responsibilities.

However, we are concerned here with capturing the AS IS so it is reasonable to capture responsibilities but in such a way that the flow is not clouded. The use of colours to denote responsibilities least interferes with the depiction of the flow and is less likely to inhibit organisational changes.

Adding activity flowchart information

Another question that arises is whether you plot left to right or top to bottom. You may be able to get more on a page by going left to right, then down and left to right again, than if you go top to bottom. Top to bottom is the convention for IT flowcharts, which are done at the task level and that method is advocated later for procedural and business requirements flowcharting.

The following example, which is a simplified flow for the allocation of supervisors for postgraduate students at a university, demonstrates these two points (you will not see colour, just shading).

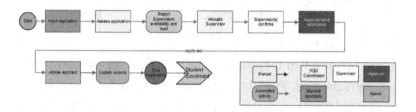

This chart contains responsibility information using colour, hence the key at the bottom right. Notice how the flow goes across then down and across again. Notice also the insertion of an 'End' symbol for the process before showing the connection to the next process, the latter is not necessary but provides additional information to the reader.

'Start' (or 'Go') and 'End' (or 'Stop') circles are added at the beginning and end of flows, this is good practice so it is easy to see entry and exit points. There may be more than one of each depending upon differing classifications or conditions. It also means that every box on the chart has at least one arrow in and one arrow out, so the flow is complete; do not leave boxes 'hanging'. Notice also the statements of condition on the arrows where the flow branches.

Different shape boxes may be used to denote different types of activities. For example in the diagram above, all square corner box activities are conducted 'on screen' by human keyboard input, however the oval boxes denote that the activity is automated by the system.

Swim lanes

Another flowchart format separates tasks into columns, or 'swim lanes' according to responsibility, see an example right. Swim lanes are better used

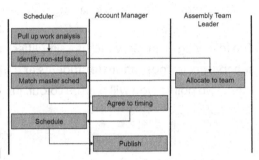

at the task level. In the example the first six tasks are part of the activity 'Schedule'. 'Publish' may be a separate activity as it results in an interim output, or it can be interpreted as the last task in the activity 'Schedule', more information is required to determine which is correct.

I do not advocate using swim lanes at the activity level because people immediately focus on their column and lose sight of the overall process and the process flow; however, the swim lanes format may be useful at the procedural, or business requirements level.

Activity flowcharting workshops

Do not be tempted to draw flowcharts on your own. The best information comes from those who do the work and getting people together means that different perspectives can be ironed out as you go.

It is important to get the right people to a workshop, and this needs to be planned carefully and checked the first time the group meet. If you reach a part of the process and no-one in the room has direct knowledge of it then defer charting that part until you can get a knowledgeable person to a later workshop.

In practice this means you will have a mixture of managers and working staff in the room together.

The workshop needs to be facilitated by a business process specialist who can facilitate workshops so as to get the best and complete information. That person can provide final charts from a diagramming tool after the session.

Distinguishing levels

One of the difficulties that many process teams meet is deciding at what level they are working, is it activity or task or even subprocess level? It is important to keep the definition of each of these levels in mind to determine which level is being worked on, but even that may not be enough. In practice, experience is what enables determination of the level. However, whilst setting levels becomes relatively intuitive with experience, even highly experienced people can get it wrong!

It is not an issue to get too concerned about, take a view and move on. If it turns out that the wrong level was assumed the correct level can be defined later on when it becomes clear from the rest of the process design that the level of the section concerned is out of alignment. It is making mistakes that develops the experience and a 'feel' for what is right.

Activity analyses

If you cannot get a workshop together and must collect information by interview you can build a straw man flowchart by piecing together the information you collect in interview. To do this you need to collect the following information:

Activity	Ref	% time	Capacity	Through-put	Work rate (1–5)	Info/ work From	Info/ work To	Comments
Allocate work	3	60%	24	20	3	Orders	Service	T. range 15–30. Works up to 10% OT

When you start you will not know what all the activities in the end-to end process are, so you have to find your way. You can do this by collecting the To and From information as this leads you to connected roles and then to the activities they perform. Add the activity references after you have assembled the process flow.

If you know the capacity and what throughput they are currently achieving you can begin to see where there are resource constraints. But people work at different work rates, so some sort of work rate assessment is a refinement, for example, assess someone on a scale of 1 to 5. You may do this for all their work or for particular activities, the person's manager can help you with this.

It becomes more difficult to assess activity percentages, resource allocations and capacities when work is cyclical. For example a university works on a semester and yearly cycle. People do different work at different times of the year. To deal with this it is necessary to split the year into phases and collect information for each phase.

Work can vary over time, in the example the activity is reported to vary from 15 to 30. The capacity is 24 and the average throughput is 20, so the individual must either increase their activity from 60% to 90% or work overtime (% time and throughput is for normal time). In the example the individual says they can work up to 10% overtime, so % time can go to 66%, or more if another activity time is reduced, or work rate can go up, etc. The variables in this simple, typical example are numerous and some conclusions need to be stated in comments if the information is to be used for resource planning later on. This information is valuable as process measures for the AS IS, which we will discuss in more detail later.

It is quite normal for interviewees to talk in terms of tasks they perform. You can collect this information but you need to assemble tasks into activities.

You need to assign % time to collaborative work, for example, cover reception during lunchtime. This is then added to the 'Provide reception service' activity.

If a process is worked out in workshops it may be necessary to interview individuals later to collect the resource consumption times. This will provide a useful check that everything has been covered in the process flowchart.

Process matrices

To ensure full communication to all members of an audience it is a good rule to present information three ways. Process Matrices are our second presentation method. Not everyone likes flowcharts, those with a bent towards spreadsheets like matrices. Matrices are also another way of cross-checking process flow-charts.

Matrices also enable additional information to be collected, here is an example:

Process:				User:		Version	Date	
Code	Activity	Predecessor	Trigger	Resp.	Techniques/ tools/ docs	Completion condition	Output/ deliverable	Successor

The matrices are similar to the activity analyses but contain information about the activity flow rather than resource consumption. However, both contain activity predecessors and successors (or From, To) information so can be directly related to the workflow chart. In the case of the matrices however, the information can be gathered in workshops, or more likely prepared by the facilitator between workshops and ratified in the workshops.

Process Matrices are not essential, but they are useful and provide a good check on process charts.

Process profiles

A Process Profile is a formatted document using Word or another word processor that allows category boxes to expand as they are filled in—which should be done on screen in workshop. An example Process Profile form is shown in Appendix D.

The Process Profile is started during the AS IS phase and reviewed and added to right up until go-live. A Process Profiles is an abbreviated document, a template that is valuable in encouraging discussion and raising the level of focus to the end-to-end process level.

The Process Profile is an important part of the methodology and should not be missed out, it is a thinking tool which encourages stakeholders to think carefully about the issues with the process, why the process exists and what the objectives of the process are. It is the beginning of getting participants to think outside of the present process and to strive for a process that is better than all existing variants of the process.

Process definition

A process definition is an expanded Process Profile laid out with sections rather than fields. An example is shown in Appendix E. Which sections to use are optional, not all of those shown in the example are likely to be used, the team needs to pick a sections list and use it consistently.

Templates

Information can be presented in different formats. An example of a Subprocess/Activity template is shown in Appendix F and this block style can be used for any level of profile and just lays out the profile information in a different format.

CHAPTER 5

Process Innovation — Realising the Potential

Process innovation means fundamentally changing the way things are done, not just refining what is done—the latter is what is meant by process improvement.

It is usual for a process that has not been previously worked on end-to-end to have great potential for radical redesign with significant business benefits.

Process innovation vs process improvement

Process improvement is evolutionary, it is gradual and progressive. Process innovation is revolutionary, it creates a disconnect between the old and new process, it is about strategic realignment. Both are valuable, but completion of process innovation is the starting point for process improvement.

After completing process innovation there will always be ways of further improving the process.

The techniques for process innovation are different to those for process improvement and they are each done by different groups; innovation is done in programs/projects, improvement during operations. That is not to exclude innovation during operation or improvement during a project, but each has its primary purpose.

Process innovation is not a new idea, in the 1980s and 90s there was a major management movement called 'Business Process Reengineering', or BPR. Some important lessons were learned from the BPR experience, which inform best practice for today's BPM.

Lessons from the BPR era

The BPR era ran from the mid 1980s to the mid 1990s. Studies in the early 1990s said 70% of process reengineering programs had actually made things worse.[xvii]

BPR became a management fad; no CEO could afford not to be seen doing it. The problem was with the way it was done not with the idea; BPR became synonymous with downsizing and the downsizing caused confusion, resentment and big mistakes.

The reasons for this are now well understood. Companies called in outside experts and information technologists, who, encouraged by the gurus of BPR, proceeded to ignore what had gone before and designed new processes on a blank sheet of paper, implemented them, collected their fees and walked away.

This approach ignored the culture and actual complexity, did not tap into conventional wisdom, and because they were not personally impacted, did not take account of the people. Any real gains were made from moving from a functional to an enterprise view.

Later on, senior managements were just closing doors and picking a percentage of people by which they had to downsize, often to meet head office's demands, then working through their staff lists and picking people based on the managers' assessments, who were then declared redundant. There was no process analysis, no work analysis of any sort, just arbitrary headcount reduction. This was not BPR, just downsizing.

Eventually the BPR era was overtaken by next great folly—Y2K (year 2000), when computer systems that had date fields which did not take account of the change in the millennium were expected to fail; therefore, huge effort and cost was expended updating these systems.

The lessons learned from the BPR era were:

It's all about people.

People are not stupid; they know what is going on. If they are not told what is going on behind closed doors they will invent it and the rumours will run wild.

So be upfront and candid about process work, and communicate, communicate, communicate. If the new processes are going to result in people being excess to requirements in their old roles, provide reassignment mechanisms. Above all, be ethical and fair. In the main, people will respond to an honest communication and explanation of what the organisation is doing and what the business imperative is that is driving it. If the imperative is not strong enough, why are you doing it?

The principles of good change management are essential to process programs. The techniques and methods aid the innovation, but people have to make it work. It really is all about people.

It's about insight

Much of the work that looked at current practices, if at all, relied on managers' perceptions of what was going on. These were often proved inaccurate and idealised.

Understand the process as it exists, not as the managers believe it is. That is not being derogatory to the managers, it is just the reality. This means talking to the people who know, the people doing the work. Insight is essential because it is more complicated than you think, the smallest omission can cause a big breakdown and loss of confidence later on.

Focus upstream

Many BPR projects were focused on the bowels of the organisation and when completed did not realise the expected savings. This was mostly due to the theory of constraints not being understood but also because there was inadequate linkage to customer value.

We know that processes are about delivery of value to customers, so end with the customer. We also know to focus on the constraint. Now add to that—focus on the activities nearest the customer in terms of prioritisation, because they will yield the largest dividends.

Take the customer's perspective

Many BPR projects did not even talk to the customer; in fact the people they did talk to were often senior functional managers and so functional objectives were picked up. Consequently what is important to the customer was not considered and the organisational view was poorly interpreted.

Make the organisation easy to do business with; do not allow internal organisational differences and functional boundaries to get in the way. Talk to the customer about how the organisation could improve its process, the conversation may be revealing, and the customer will appreciate being consulted.

Sales people may fear this sort of conversation as they believe it may build unrealistic expectations, but expectations can be managed by being realistic with the customer about what can be achieved.

Eliminate non-value work

By taking a blank sheet of paper BPR consultants were able to show significant reduction in resource needs. However, these were spurious, as necessary work was missed and not accounted for, and afterward implementation processes were altered again to pick up missing tasks.

If an end-to-end perspective is taken and a solid understanding of the value being created by a process is kept in mind then it soon becomes obvious if an activity is not adding value. Such activities are there because 'we've always done it this way', things have changed but no-one has changed the process. They may be there because of functional reasons which really do not add value to the organisation. Or they may even be there for political or status reasons.

Process focus changes organisational structures

Many BPR projects failed on implementation. Functional managers mounted such a backlash that CEOs backed away from the consultants' recommendations and tried to implement the processes using current organisational structures. Once the functional managers had the upper hand they were able to modify processes to their own preferences and the enterprise view was eroded.

Power moves from function to process, because processes align with customers. This means functions must support processes. Functions are still important as they are responsible for skills, professionalism and competencies, but business processes have the greater authority. This can be a huge paradigm shift for some organisations. It has the potential to create disruptive turf wars and considerable angst amongst the management cadre. This may not be evident until after processes have been redesigned and are about to be implemented. This is the primary reason that the process program must have the proactive support of the CEO or senior manager to whom the functional management report.

It has to be said that some organisations lack the will to make the shift and attempt some form of mixed model, resulting in confusion and political infighting. We will consider these issues in a later chapter.

Be bold

It is never good consulting practice to produce a surprise for the customer that the CEO does not know is coming. The BPR consultants presented finalised processes and were surprised when not everyone applauded.

There is a very good chance that innovated processes will be a surprise to someone. If no-one shows surprise then either the doubters are keeping quiet seeing how things go or there is no real innovation. Lack of innovation either arises from an inadequate process design process or a lack of boldness in ideas. Both of these come down to methods and facilitation.

Be prepared to let go of sacred cows. This is really about the method, how to free up a group of people to allow themselves to think of the process in new ways, to be bold with their ideas and not think they will be belittled. Once the new ideas are on the table then later on is the time to discuss whether they are feasible and worth adopting.

Consult stakeholders

If innovated processes are well communicated to stakeholders before a system is finalised, doubters have a chance to air their issues and to feel they are being consulted. This enables both sides to work out what to do, often doubters will come round if they are listened to and are given good reasons for the new design, or there may be a modification that does not detract from the new design but settles the doubters' issue and there is time to make the change.

Be sure, test first

The BPR assumption was that the new process was right and could be implemented straight away, and consultants often do not want to do implementation, they leave that to the organisation. In consequence, inadequate processes were implemented without testing or piloting and so were quickly brought into disrepute when issues arose.

Do not be so impressed with your new process that you rush it into operation. You must test it and pilot it first. In these modes people know you are trying to find errors and improvements and will be forgiving. Once it is in production they expect it to be right, if it is not it will quickly fall into disrepute and you may fail. In particular, make sure all stakeholders have a chance to see what is proposed and to provide their reaction and input.

It's the start of the journey, not the end

Organisations were sold the idea that once BPR was complete the organisation was good for years, a bit like surgery. However, organisations do not self-heal unless they are set up that way. The way to set it up is to implement process improvement processes once process innovation is complete.

By the time process innovation has been implemented improvements are already obvious, and have had to be put back to a later process version in order to put the first version into operation. Businesses are dynamic, their environment is constantly changing, technology is changing, their customers are changing, everything is changing. They cannot stand still. There will always be ways to improve the process as things change, so a process is required to ensure process improvement occurs.

Process innovation is a driver for cultural change for the better

Because process is focused on the customer it makes people in the organisation look in the same direction, outward toward the customer, instead of internally at each other. This fosters collaboration and better understanding of what other people need and reduced friction and internal political intrigues.

BPM in the 21st Century.

BPM has developed in this century as a vital strategic tool for organisational reform; it takes on board the lessons from the BPR era and has evolved to deal with the new organisational drivers that have emerged since.

The new strategic drivers are:

Flattened organisation

The days of having many supervision and management levels are numbered, for some organisations they are already past. The cost of many levels is prohibitive. Modern education and social trends mean people are less inclined to accept direction without question; people want to be involved in decisions which affect their work. This has led to the greater use of work teams within flatter organisation structures and wider spans of control for managers.

The concept of a supervisor or manager constantly directing work, and no-one being able to do anything without a directive, has evolved into managers overseeing work and ensuring employees have adequate education and training to do the work without continuous supervision.

In this scenario senior management requires assurance that staff will complete their tasks within acceptable parameters. Processes specify the guidelines and boundaries within which people do their work. However, processes do not include task instructions, so if senior management requires procedural control then a system written at task level is necessary. The process project may include writing the business requirements at the task level, so procedural rules and policies can be implemented.

The question here is what level of central control is optimal and how much should be delegated. The process design process does require task instructions to be drafted by those doing the work, so the principles of decentralisation are recognised; however, this may make the organisation less flexible and self-adapting than implementing a process at the activity level.

BPM tries hard to make implemented systems easy to alter and so inflexibility may not be a problem; how responsive they are depends on whether business users can make changes directly in the system model, or if IT must make changes. Ultimately, this will come down to what culture the senior leaders want in the organisation, and what strategies for BPM they adopt.

eEverything, the spread of computerisation

Computing power is everywhere in business today. Large organisations have long had dedicated core business systems and tailored functional utilities. These systems manage internal data and many activities are automated (transactions are completed without human intervention). These systems automate tasks or activities (sometimes called 'services' by IT) but not usually end-to-end processes. The user sees them as database systems. Database systems are passive and require users to select the task to complete and the user inputs or retrieves information from databases. These systems have been mostly internal to their organisations but internet technology has changed that assumption.

Internet technologies have expanded the sense of electronic connectedness to the outside world, with access to information on demand and the ability for customers and suppliers to deal with organisations electronically.

The first industry to break through in this regard was the financial services industry and we are all now used to online banking, invoice payment, tax returns, welfare payments, and other financial transactions which combine individual occasional use using internet browsers with automation using large systems within the organisations to handle the large volumes of transactions. But even today major banks are still working on moving to new flexible computing systems from core systems that date back decades. The new systems provide automated task completion once the user provides the necessary input.

People have become accustomed to these systems and have come to expect instantaneous responses *and* personalised service. Tax return systems are examples of how these systems have grown in complexity and provide online forms for users that allow for individual circumstances, whilst at the same time, data collection costs for the tax authorities are reduced and their turn-around time much improved.

The next big wave was non-financial industry business to business (B2B) systems and online shopping or business to customer (B2C) systems, which are still developing and growing rapidly. These systems have expanded the functionality of online financial transactions by adding catalogue display, product selection and invoicing to online payment. They are then integrated with internal order and dispatch systems and so are real end-to-end systems which are highly automated. These systems scale, they are available for use by a one person trading operation right up to the major retail chains. Note that the pattern of usage allows complete automation (with exceptions) due to the repetitious nature of the transactions, but offer great flexibility to the user by presenting many options linked into their large databases. These systems are especially convenient for retail customers and retail suppliers because they connect to the large banking systems for payments through secure 'gateways'.

The large systems handle enormous quantities of repetitious transactions but they are very expensive to develop and maintain. The need for greater efficiency drives the need for lower volume online systems that are used occasionally by employees, customers and other users, and are complex in nature—that is, the exact outcome may not be predictable in advance. A lot of this sort of work is still being done by users using personal computer desktop software and email, even paper. The work typically depends upon human decision-making as there is a need for interpretation of rules and policies. However, the scale is such that the cost of very large scale systems for individual processes cannot be justified.

Many forms that start these processes have been put up on the internet for customers and users to complete and a form is sent to the organisation electronically. This gives an illusion of automation but in fact the form may be printed out in the organisation and processed as before or passed around internally by email, or at best, filed in a database system for retrieval by users. The result is slow, inefficient and inconsistent responses by the organisation that do not match the user's perception of eEverything.

Workflow technology is a means of providing the level of eEverything that users expect for people-centric processes, but at a lower cost than traditional large volume systems. Many of the lower volume processes can be automated or at least put online using this technology. The addition of process modeling and real-time process management to workflow management, together with more functionality for workflow management, has led to the new class of system called Business Process Management Systems (BPMS).

Workflow management replaces supervision

With the removal of supervision, management was concerned that quality and consistency, and the work-rate that supervisors used to enforce, would diminish. Systems that manage workflow were developed as a direct result of this removal of supervision, and to meet expectations of faster service and the need for cost reduction.

Good workflow brings work to the worker, automates some tasks, provides limited options to ensure good governance, and provides metrics on the efficiency of the process. Any potential adverse impact of removal of supervision has been overcome.

Moving from functional activities and subprocesses to processes

Processes develop piecemeal over time, task by task, function by function and are often not recognised as processes—merely as things that need to done individually. Database systems encouraged organisations to view workflow as just for individual functions or tasks, or services. Each bit of functionality was examined, the short flow just for that function documented, and implemented as a database system command or option. This enabled individual functions to develop systems just for their part of the business. Often all that was done was to computerise what was already being done with some process improvement. As the process was not recognised end-to-end there was no attempt at process innovation.

The result has been fragmented processes that are not optimised for the organisation as a whole, they are, in fact, just disconnected subprocesses. Subprocesses may include tasks and activities that do not benefit the organisation, but are seen as important by the function that developed them.

Need to eliminate non-productive work

By innovating the process end-to-end, non-productive work becomes easier to identify and remove in a way that has not necessarily happened with the introduction of database systems.

The IT industry has introduced the concept of 'services' which can have the same impact if each service is seen as a stand-alone system function the same as with database systems. However, if the services are defined within a Service Oriented Architecture (SOA) then this may approximate to a process architecture and result in more of a process view that will encourage elimination of non-productive work.

Workflow integration, elimination of errors and duplication

Errors occur when data is transcribed from one document to another or from one system to another. Transcription is also time-consuming and wasteful of resource—the work adds no value. Transferring data from one system to another also results in duplication of data. At the time of transcription the data are equal, but when one system updates the data without reference to the other data they become unequal and this can lead to confusion and errors. The IT industry has a concept called 'normalisation', which means systems are written in such a way that a piece of data is only held in one place and all systems refer to that one place for that data. This requires integration of systems. Complex integration becomes very expensive to develop and maintain.

Workflow can be an integration mechanism. One process may collect and store a piece of data in a database, another process may retrieve the piece of data from the database and use it. Each process knows where to go for the data, but stands alone as a process. The database may be an existing database or a new one used by the BPMS, it is irrelevant for the BPMS, so long as the workflow knows where to go for its data.

Thus, using workflow as an integration mechanism avoids the cost of redeveloping existing large systems, the full benefit of normalisation is achieved and workflow management is implemented.

Customer value improvement

The customer wants to receive the value of what it purchases at a reasonable price and in a reasonable time with the minimum of difficulty. And value will change over time. It is up to the organisation to understand what the customer considers to be value and work out the best way of delivering that value at a profit, or an acceptable cost in the case of publicly funded organisations.

Because processes are oriented on delivery of value to the customer they orient staff towards the customer. This eliminates a lot of internal politicking and resource wastage. Improvement in the customer value becomes an easily understood common goal and lends a sense of purpose to the organisation that motivates people and results in increasing efficiency and staff and customer satisfaction.

Dealing with complexity

Complexity cannot be managed centrally, there are too many variables to handle. It requires those with the best knowledge of each individual situation to deal with that situation, and those people are the front-line people. In order for management to have confidence that the front-line people will make the right decision commercially and according to governance requirements, the front-line people need to have easily assimilated, context–relevant guidance.

Processes provide this guidance and the business rules embedded in the workflow are in fact micro-policy and therefore provide governance confidence. Moreover, workflow system records are very comprehensive and provide excellent audit trials if required. Decentralised decision-making is the way to deal with complexity.

Need for speed

Modern organisations are constantly under pressure to react faster, computerisation has brought an expectation of immediate response. This is only possible with decentralised decision making and rapid systems response. Workflow is part of the range of computing systems that enable rapid response.

Roles and processes

Contribution, collaboration, not job task list

Under traditional hierarchical organisation people are given a job description that lists the tasks they must accomplish. They are responsible for those tasks and are measured and rewarded based on their performance in completing the specified tasks, and those alone. This encourages people to just focus on their own tasks and to shift the blame if something goes wrong. Collaboration tends to only arise if it supports self-interest and most people do not have time to help others, although those with a sociable or altruistic nature may do so.

On the other hand, if job descriptions are written to emphasise contribution to end-to-end processes and measurement is based on process output, even though a person may in fact be doing the same work, they will become more collaborative and think about ways in which the overall process can be improved and how collectively they can improve their working lives. This is how roles are defined for processes and cross-functional views are opened up enabling real understanding of what other people do.

Managing performance

Most people come to work to do a good job, there is no satisfaction in doing a bad job. Again, most people enjoy being part of a team rather than struggling on their own. Another benefit of forming process teams is that teams will often manage poor performance by an individual without management intervention, because poor performance affects their collective process performance. Team members will train a slow performer and if they do not improve will find a way to remove them from the team.

CHAPTER **6**

Creating the TO BE process design — Innovating the Process

Designing the new process, system and procedure is done in three steps, previously illustrated as the latter three steps in this diagram:

1. The TO BE is the straightforward business process at activity level, without consideration of technology.
2. The SYSTEM design takes the TO BE and improves it using BPMS technology assumptions, but it is still at the activity level. Once teams have completed one or more processes the TO BE and SYSTEM designs are often amalgamated as the team understands the capabilities of the BPMS technology, so the TO BE incorporates BPMS assumptions. The strategic process innovation is most often done during the design of the TO BE and SYSTEM.
3. The Business Requirements take the TO BE/SYSTEM down to the procedural/task level. A process cannot be implemented without completing procedural detail and a BPMS cannot be

configured without completing the task level. The procedural and task details are developed together.

This chapter is about the TO BE step, but many of the points made apply to the SYSTEM step as well.

The TO BE team

Firstly, who are the people that work on the TO BE?

See the previous discussions of the program and project roles; picking the right people for these roles is crucial to the success of the program.

The designing of the TO BE (and SYSTEM if it is done separately) is best undertaken by the program team, involving, as necessary, some of the people who do the work. These phases do not take up a lot of time.

Later on, when skills have been acquired and formats have settled down, project teams may complete the TO BE/SYSTEM, but only if the project leaders have the necessary open leadership style and a direct interest in achieving the business benefits, and the project teams include a BPM specialist or consultant who has also been involved with the program team. If projects are being run by project or IT managers, rather than business leaders, then the program team should definitely complete the AS IS and TO BE/SYSTEM maps.

An example of this approach is that the TO BE (and SYSTEM) is undertaken by a 'Transformation' team which is a highly experienced/ senior group of business people that are implementing a business strategy of defined change to the organisation. Such a team must be sure to avoid the pitfalls experienced during the BPR Era discussed earlier—they should not assume they can just design a new process in isolation as an intellectual exercise.

Pitfalls to avoid

Before we get to what enables process innovation, let us first review what is almost certain to kill it.

Single person solutions

The Project Leader and/or the BPM Specialist must not develop process solutions and present them to the team for acceptance; this is to remove the power of the group's knowledge and the advantages of the brainstorming process. No matter how skilled the person is this will lead to a more limited result. The same applies if an individual in the team tries to force their solution on the group. The Leader must prevent this. If it is the Leader dominating the team and drowning out the will of other team members to come up with ideas then the BPM Specialist needs to have a quiet word with him/her or refer the matter to the Project Owner!

Team isolation

Similarly, one of the traps of process design is for a person or team to go into a room, close the door, and later emerge with a fully designed process. This approach always results in a sub-optimised design because, in the absence of feedback, the knowledge applied is limited. Businesses are complex and processes need to embody the full relevant knowledge available within the organisation.

Incremental improvements

Many process projects never know what opportunities they miss. The team develops an approach which takes the current process and finds improvements, resulting in changes that stakeholders feel indicate success. But often the original strategic objectives are not achieved in full. This is particularly so with IT-system-driven process work (not that IT has to have this impact, but experience indicates that it often does).

Innovation is not the same as incremental improvements. Innovation is about putting things together is new ways, for example: changing the sequence; grouping activities differently; taking out some activities; taking out some activities for some instances that can be fast-tracked, just doing things differently.

The best innovation usually comes from designing the process from end-to-end with a focus on end value. However, BPMS technology also offers new innovative opportunities, for example: have the system make decisions based on rules where previously the user had to read policies and then decide; start multiple activities in parallel; bring input forward so the process is not held up later; provide fast track routing dependent upon input; proactively queue tasks and advise performers.

Incremental improvements tend to be done at the task level; these improvements can be teased out during the business requirements phase.

Captured by the IT application

Designing processes as part of an IT system project can encourage focus on business requirements, that is the task level, which can be an impediment to process innovation. If there is a desire to use the modeller in a BPMS the impediment can be avoided if the process modelling module is stand-alone (albeit can provide input to other modules), as this enables easy design at the activity level and is intuitive for business people. Then it is up to the BPM Specialist or Project Leader to keep the design at the activity level.

Many process projects are seen as IT system projects. The first activity is the selection of the system vendor and application. The process is then defined using the new system's tools. This is to constrain thinking by the workflow included in the system, the system will be configurable but still it will influence how the process is defined. The most critical limitation is that the system is configured at the task level, limiting the likelihood of real process innovation.

Even if an IT application is preferred, or is even already installed, it is still best to define the process before completing the business requirements in accordance with the IT application. Then it is quite clear what the gap is between the optimum process and what is being specified. Defining the gap will enable decisions to be made about whether to provide unique subroutines or coding which will be necessary to implement the preferred process.

Too much detail in the early phases

Another trap is to focus on the detail too soon. It is important to get people to think 'out of the rut' of their everyday involvement. This is where a skilled facilitator is essential. The facilitator ensures that the conversation is initially broad-ranging and open to enable the team to see some visionary ideas about what can be done to really improve the process. The facilitator needs to stop people who are detail focused (not a bad characteristic per se, but one that is not helpful in the innovation phase) getting control of the conversation because of their natural inclination to drive down to detail at the task level. The facilitator needs to bring the conversation back to the activity level.

This is not to say that useful task information should be totally ignored, if it relates to the value the activity creates it may be appropriate to add explanatory task information as activity notes to activities.

Wrong level of analysis

The levels of analysis need to be well understood by the team:

Many organisations make the mistake of analysing the AS IS at too low a level, the task level. This is not necessary and takes up a lot of time. In fact it is better not to analyse the AS IS and TO BE at a low level because the sight of the wood is lost for the trees. That is, the chances of process innovation are greatly reduced. People become absorbed with the fine detail of task work at this level and tend to be defensive about how they do their own work. This leads to entrenched positions and difficulty reaching agreement. The result can be a patchwork of existing practices with some improvements. However, if teams are focused on the activity level the focus is not on 'how' the work is done, but on 'what' needs doing and 'when' it is best done. This encourages innovative thinking.

It is not always easy for team members to work out what is an activity and what is a task, this comes with practice, but sometimes it may be necessary to reassess the level of a particular activity/task as the rest of the process is worked out.

The other consideration is to ensure that there is real value being created by what is being done.

Using complicated tools in workshops

It is this trap that results in the suggestion not to use IT 'design' tools in innovation workshops. IT tools can map processes at the activity level but it is so easy to drill down to the task level that people want to do that all the time. A skilled IT tool user may be able to contain the conversation to the activity level but my preference is to use a whiteboard which cannot drill down and put the design into a tool later.

Not rigorously ensuring value creation

Many activities are undertaken because of corporate rules and requirements. These may be valid, for example, an approval may be required in support of governance principles set by the Board, but they may reflect a local management preference based on maintaining control, such as an approval of work done. The question becomes, 'Does the activity add value for the organisation?' if not, is it necessary?

The value will either benefit the customer directly or benefit the organisation in some way that enables the organisation to function efficiently and effectively, which will in turn improve the value to the customer.

Customer value

Customer value is created if what is worked is improved in a way that the customer recognises as of benefit. This may be the completion of an interim deliverable or some change of state. Note that this definition aligns with the definition of an activity and is one of the reasons we do the design at the activity level.

Genuine corporate value

It can be surprising how many activities are undertaken because 'we have always done it this way'. People do not have time to examine the process if they are working hard on producing service or product. Processes are built up over time and tend to be functionally defined as stand-alone activities that each function must complete—an overall process view has not been taken. It is taking the overall organisational perspective that enables processes to be fundamentally improved.

Experience indicates that front-line people often have the best ideas as to how to streamline activities, because it will make their lives easier. The people who raise objections to streamlining are the managers who can see their power and influence fading as the process team starts to work end to end and communicate horizontally instead of referring to their managers all the time.

What this means is that supposedly corporate value is often functional and managerial value, which is not of genuine corporate value and can be eliminated.

Critical success factors

Having considered some of the pitfalls above, how do we actually ensure that a process is innovated, what is it that results in genuine innovation rather than just improvement?

Process innovation—which is the spark applied to collective knowledge to create something better than can be produced by any individual—needs to be built on multi-dimensional insight. This means that contention and argument, arising from different perspectives and goals, are part of the process. *The only remedy is to come up with a design that is better than any single existing design or idea, so that all can buy into the solution.* This may require negotiation and trade-offs, but again, that is part of the process. Too heavy a hand on the design process kills innovation as it is imposing an individual's viewpoint.

It all comes down to creating a workshop environment in which people build on each other's ideas.

There are a number of critical success factors (CSFs) the facilitator/ leader must take account of which experience has proved are important for process innovation:

- The team has settled down, is open in its discussions, and hierarchy has become less important (to say it is no longer influential at all is unrealistic).

  The Program Owner and the BPM Specialist set the stage for the program team and the program team sets the stage for each process project. In both cases it is about describing the business drivers and strategy and creating a vision of what can be achieved and what it means for the business.

- A level of excitement and expectation has developed amongst stakeholders and the team in response to the realisation of the potential benefits of the program.

  This comes from recognising that innovation is possible, and what can be achieved is of strategic importance to the organisation and how it will make working life less frustrating and more satisfying for the stakeholders. The Program Owner and BPM Specialist are responsible for painting the picture of what can be achieved.

- The program team has discussed and documented clear business goals and objectives for the program. Principles are also a useful tool, particularly for not-for-profit organisations.

Rules for the team and program or project are agreed, these help reduce any hierarchical impediments to the workings of the team.

- Team goals include producing a solution that is better than all of the current practices.

This is a critical point, teams often get stuck in a mode of pushing their practice as the best when in fact they should be participating in coming up with a new solution that is better for everyone. If not better for everyone then at least different groups should negotiate trade-offs allowing solution consensus.

- A 'sense-making' approach is used, particularly in program work, so that common sense prevails over tradition and political influence.

People are used to working under pressure to do something, they are action-oriented. This is good in one sense but it can encourage people to charge off in the wrong direction without challenging assumptions or acquiring enough information. Consciously demanding that common sense is applied enables people to challenge old assumptions and habits.

- Team members discover, if they did not already know, that workshops require give and take.

  People are used to advocating their position whereas in a workshop dialogue is necessary. This means putting aside preconceived viewpoints before engaging in the discussion and displaying an openness to other people's ideas and needs.

- At the same time, stakeholder representative team members ensure that their area of interest is properly taken into account, if necessary negotiating trade-offs.

  Good solutions need to take account of all perspectives and objectives and sometimes these conflict. To reconcile differences people need to be able to trade accepting that someone else's need is valid and will be taken into account in order to have their own need accepted as well. At the same time, if people engage in open discussion they may be able to re-examine some of their assumptions and accept that the new solution may remove or modify their need.

- A facilitator creates the right team dynamics, challenges the participants to innovate, understands BPM and manages the mechanics of process workshops.

  This is the role of the BPM Specialist, who may also be the Program Manager. The person needs the experience, knowledge and skills to conduct productive process workshops. Without such a person the workshops may become confrontational or apathetic and therefore unproductive.

Occasionally, even with the right facilitator, the politics within the group are so poor that different people in the group try to gain ascendency and set their own agenda. If this is the case the facilitator needs to discuss the situation with the Program Owner and it may be necessary to disband the team and form a new one.

- The facilitator manages group interaction, probes the sacred cows and entrenched ideas and challenges the group to build a better process.

Process innovation can be emasculated by sacred cows and entrenched ideas. The facilitator needs to be sufficiently outside the day-to-day politics to be able to challenge conventional organisational thinking. The Process Owner is responsible for ensuring the program has an effective workshop facilitator and leader.

- The development process includes thinking tools and methods that encourage team members to start thinking 'out of the rut' and at a higher level than their day-to-day tasks.

The Process Profile, Value Diagram and the flowcharts themselves are examples of thinking tools I have already recommended. There are other thinking tools such as System Diagrams, Decision Trees, Conflict Resolution Diagrams, Mind Maps, Fishbone Diagrams, Cause and Effect Diagrams and de Bono's Six Thinking Hats that can assist the thinking processes of a workshop group. However, do not get carried away with fun activities at the expense of progress! The facilitator needs to pick the minimum number of thinking tools to generate the right level of interaction in the group.

- Mapping and design work is done at the activity level, not task level.

  This encourages team members to lift their sights. It is easy to be sucked down to the task level because this is the level that people work at and so it is natural for them to want to talk about that level. It is up to the facilitator to lead the team into staying at the activity level. Task detail can be discussed but it should be documented as notes to activities not as flow boxes in the same way as activities.

- Finish the AS IS before starting the TO BE. Map the AS IS first to understand all of the process issues, and if it is done at the activity level it does not take long.

  Some consultants are inclined to think they know what makes a good process and that the best approach is to start with a blank sheet of paper and not be influenced by what currently happens. Also, as soon as a process team starts working on the AS IS they can immediately see ways of improving the process, so if they are not constrained they will go straight into designing the TO BE.

- Use simple BPM tools during workshops to enable immediate understanding by business participants.

  Tools must be intuitive and transparent so that team members focus on the process discussion. Some facilitators and even team members get fascinated with using complicated IT tools and lose sight of the business objectives. More complicated IT tools can be used between workshops to document workshop results.

- Develop an approach that is flexible and can use different tools for different processes.

  Some processes need tools that others do not need, but more importantly, personalities change between projects and different tools and methods may suit different teams. This is intensive people work and the facilitator needs to pick what is likely to produce the best results for any one team.

- Despite the above, there needs to be enough common publishing standards and tools and methods across the program so that documentation is consistent and users and stakeholders readily understand content.

  Common language, presentation and documentation sets enable efficiency as the program progresses. The secret lies in not imposing them in a bureaucratic or policeman-like manner but offering them when they are applicable.

  This can be amongst the offerings of an Enterprise Program Office (EPO) or Project Management Office (PMO).

Critical path and dwell time; constraint activities

As well as the above CSFs there is a critical concept that often enables dramatic reductions in process cycle times.

The concept of the critical path is well known in project planning. The critical path defines the sequence of activities that define the shortest possible time it will take to complete a project. Activities on the critical path have no 'float'—that is, no spare time—whereas other activities will not affect the duration of the project if they are late within their float time.

The Theory of Constraints was explained in Chapter 1, you may find it easier to think of the critical path as the constrained path as it is the path that constrains the process cycle time.

Consider this process:

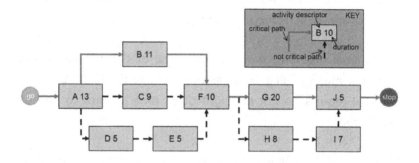

The total cycle time for the process along the critical path is 59. Other paths have float (C's duration is 9, less than B's critical 11; D/E's duration is 10 compared with B's 11; H/I's duration is 15 compared with G's 20). The process cannot be completed in under 59.

Now let us split duration between waiting time (on the arrows) and work time (in the boxes):

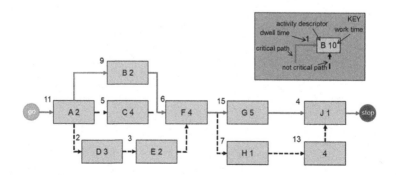

On the critical path we find that waiting, or dwell, time is 45 and work time is only 14. This means that customers wait 59 for delivery of which only 14 is critical work time. This ratio is common.

Management practice is poor at identifying dwell time because organisations primarily rely on financial reporting for management purposes. Dwell time does not consume direct resources (it may consume space costs, but they are in overheads and overheads are typically allocated on work costs), so there is no attached cost and it does not appear in financial reporting.

Operational measures may include cycle, or delivery times and customer metrics will almost certainly include them. But because financial reports do not highlight dwell time it tends to be not considered.

Reduction of dwell time by substantial percentages is usually quite easy with process projects that include computerisation, and the impact on the customer is dramatic. The value to the customer is substantial and it costs nothing and does not affect quality.

As well as enabling reduction in dwell time, applying critical path thinking to processes enables identification of constraint activities that will most benefit the process cycle time if their duration is reduced.

TO BE design subprocess

The Design TO BE subprocess looks like the next diagram:

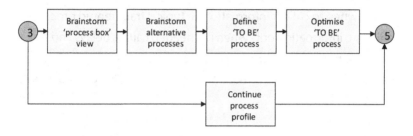

Continue process profile

The Process Profile template is shown in Appendix D. It is started during the AS IS phase but will still be incomplete and will be modified as new ideas and insights arise.

Brainstorm process box

Information acquisition is a vital part of process design, its timing and presence has a major impact on workflow efficiency. This workshop thinking tool is useful, both to look at information acquisition but also to help the team to think outside of normal process thinking.

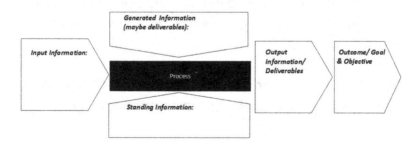

The Process Box is a tool to promote the team to think 'outside the box'; in this case, the process box which is blacked out. Talking about what information is input at the start of the process, accessed during the process and generated by the process helps the team to rethink when to collect information. In typical fragmented processes, collecting information only when it is needed causes delays and slows down the process. Completing the process box enables the team to think about collecting information as early as possible, which prevents delays later on.

The Standing Information is available for use by the process every time without change. Manuals, technical instructions, facilities and equipment information are all examples.

Generated Information must be collected or generated after the process has started and is specific to this instance of the process. This information cannot be reused whereas Standing Information can be. Generated information may be part of the process deliverables and so may be repeated in the right-hand box.

Outputs or Deliverables may be physical objects, in the example overleaf printed envelopes amongst others. However, depending on the customer contract, deliverables may include information (form designs in this example) and so also appear in Generated Information.

The Outputs/Deliverables and Outcome/Goal & Objective are included in the diagram to help focus on what the process really needs and what is superfluous.

The process itself is shown as a black or empty box, or it may include the process name, but there is no process detail of any kind.

The Process Box may look obvious but in practice it can cause extended discussion of when information is produced and is good for making people think about information in a new way.

As such, the Process Box is a thinking tool, primarily designed to promote discussion rather than because it is essential later on.

The example below is for a high volume print/mail processing operation. The Input Information is that which is available before the process starts and is unique to this instance of the process, in that, it changes every time the process is used. Typically, this is information supplied by the customer.

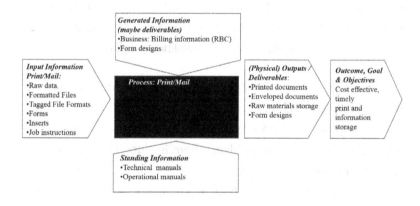

Brainstorm alternative processes

Innovating the TO BE process is about creating team interaction that triggers and builds ideas, then examining the ideas to decide which are worth including in the new design.

The people in these workshops should be a combination of people who do the work, managers and other business-oriented thinkers.

The facilitator needs to be putting up the process activities as a simple workflow diagram as they are brainstormed so that the team can see what is emerging and think about different ideas. This can be done manually on a whiteboard or using a laptop diagramming tool projected on the wall. Putting up an emerging image for all to see is crucial in getting all team members focused together on the solution rather than on each other's territorial positioning.

It does not matter if the diagram is manual and rough and ready. If a whiteboard is used the diagram can be photographed with a phone camera or if it is an electronic whiteboard the image can be printed at the end of the session. Some advanced electronic whiteboards will clean up the image on the fly. After the workshop the image can be used to generate a cleaned-up version in a desktop diagramming tool, or may even be input into a BPMS modelling tool directly.

Typically one workshop of 2 to 3 hours will generate the first end-to-end process design at activity level. The method is iterative, once a workshop has finished the participants' subconscious should be allowed to ruminate on the ideas. There is a good chance this will create further thoughts for discussion. Leave a few days then the new cleaned-up design is talked about at a follow-up workshop and the process will probably change quite a bit into a new alternative.

The following techniques are worth noting for use during the TO BE design:

- Don't accept the first solution, it is likely not yet optimised. Revisit the design on a later day and improve on it.

- 'Front-load' processes to reduce drag, collect information and do things as early as possible. The Process Box exercise will help with understanding how to do this.

- Move activities from after a fixed point to before. If certain activities are completed after a fixed point, for example, signing a contract, see whether some of them can in fact be moved to before the fixed point so that the critical path time is reduced.

- Question and remove constraints (Theory of Constraints).

- As Soon As Possible (ASAP) not As Late As Possible (ALAP). Most people schedule work on an ALAP basis so as to complete work in an order they think is the best. This often results in double handling; for example if the normal process is [receive, review, put away, take out to do, review again, do] then put away, take out and the second review are all additional time compared with an ASAP method. People find ASAP quite hard to do, they feel that they have more important things to do; however, it may mean not starting the process until they are ready to complete it.

- Talk to the customer, know where the customer value is. This is so vital. Most of the time our heads are firmly inside our own organisation and we can easily lose sight of what the customer really wants. Moreover, we may be scared of asking the customer what he/she wants because we fear we may not be able to meet their need. This is a misleading viewpoint, the customer will always prefer to be asked what is of value and know what can and cannot be delivered so that they can make an informed decision and not have false expectations.

  ○ If we do not understand what the customer values we may well do things the customer does not value and thereby incur unnecessary costs and waste time. Professionals will over-engineer because it is a matter of professional pride to produce the best possible service. This not only adds cost but also delays delivery and the customer may well prefer to get a lesser service more quickly.

- Mark activities that do not produce value, question internal 'value' that is used to justify them.

- Challenge the need for approvals and any other activities that cause delay. There is a difference between an approval for governance reasons and an approval of work. The latter is too late, the work has already been done. Good managers train their people to avoid errors and provide checking mechanisms for the people to use themselves. So check whether the work approval is not just the manager displaying their authority.

  Note that sign-offs may be required to document commitment to a plan or action, and are part of governance processes. Managers with a responsibility for a particular service do not need to sign off to show commitment to perform what is their normal responsibility—sign-offs are only required to show commitment to unique or non-conforming plans or actions.

- Mistake proof the process so that mistakes are hard to make.

- Look for external benchmarks and ways of doing things, research for ideas. The process you are designing may well occur in many other non-competitive organisations; you can save yourself a lot of time and get really good ideas by talking to these organisations before you proceed to designing the TO BE.

- Use visual controls. With modern IT systems this is a given.

- Keep output moving, design the process, and particularly the system, to pull the work along.

- Integrate the process across the organisation. If the concept of 'internal customers' exists in the organisation, move away from it. The concept enables functions to avoid having to accept the customer's requirements, rather dictate what they will produce.

- Only collect information required for that case. A process is used by many instances or cases and they will differ in detail. There is a bureaucratic tendency to ensure that every case has all of the information completed. Do not collect any information for a particular case that is not going to be used, it consumes unnecessary resources and user time.

- Bring information to the performer. Make sure that the performer does not have to go hunting for missing information, with modern systems there is no excuse for this.

- Make the process easy for users to use.

- Make the process easy for performers to perform.

Map TO BE process

The same tools used to map the AS IS are used to design the TO BE, firstly in workshop then in a diagramming tool between workshops. Once an initial version is complete in the mapping tool further improvements are made in workshop directly in the mapping tool.

Optimise TO BE

Process designs are brainstormed and iteratively improved upon as new ideas are sparked off by the workshopping. Once new ideas are exhausted a definitive version is endorsed.

Once the TO BE process design phase is complete the team's attention will turn to computerising the new process. The strategy is to complete the ideal TO BE then to consider what IT application will be used to implement the new process and if necessary amend the TO BE to become a SYSTEM design.

Before we consider the SYSTEM design an understanding of the business functionality of BPMS and process automation is needed, this is covered in the next chapter.

CHAPTER 7

Automating Processes — Using Technology to Advantage

Automation was originally used to denote control of machinery by computer instead of human operators. The word has come to also mean automatic processing of information during administrative processes by computer without human intervention.

Automation of administrative processes is done by preprogramming decisions so that they are made without human intervention. Just programming management of the workflow can be referred to as automation but is called computerisation in this book if people are doing actual work on computers instead of computers doing the work. Computerisation implies human use of a computer system.

Evolution of business process computer systems

Large systems were developed as islands of automation, finance, HR, operations, etc. Users provided input and received output as required but otherwise the systems were completely automated. These systems dealt with large volumes of repetitive operational tasks that justified the cost of automation.

Enterprise Application Integration products (EAI) were developed to enable straight-through processing between different large systems, for example, if a person earns > $xx add the person to medical scheme, details are automatically passed from the payroll application to the medical scheme application, a new membership is created and notification of the new membership issued. Straight-through processing extends automation across an organisation's set of large systems.

However, these large systems did not handle many tasks undertaken by the growing class of knowledge workers. The transaction volumes were too low to justify the considerable cost of writing dedicated large systems. Knowledge workers used desktop applications on their personal computers to do their work or used paper-based processes.

As personal computers became networked, work started to be passed around by email, information was put on network servers, and group information was taken off personal computers.

The advance of internet technologies allowed web browsers with their user–friendly interface to become the normal user interface for organisational systems, even to the extent of being grafted onto the front-end of the existing large systems.

Over time, studies indicated that the majority of transactions in organisations were 'human centric' and not processed on large systems. The need for workflow management became clear and workflow management systems emerged as a new class of application. They had the advantage of being package applications that could be configured for individual processes and so the cost was acceptable for processes with lower transaction volumes.

Workflow systems started adding business process modelling and reporting modules and the IT industry, being fond of three letter acronyms, came up with the new acronym BPM (Business Process Management) for what these new systems provided. The business community pointed out that BPM was a generic business function regardless of the use of IT applications to manage workflow and so Business Process Management System (BPMS) came to represent the computer systems built on workflow.

BPMS have become increasingly sophisticated and have added large real-time data analysis, complex event and case management processing, and use of social media and mobile devices. To market these more sophisticated BPMS, a new acronym iBPMS (Intelligent BPMS) has been coined.

BPMS and iBPMS can range from economic BPMS with workflow management and process modelling through large expensive iBPMS used by global companies and other very large organisations.

Using BPMS

Few processes are not in some way associated with a computer system. Today most business processes are designed with process automation in mind.

Computer systems can deliver major increases in process speed, availability, usability and accuracy and computer systems enable process designs that cannot be handled manually. They also enable automatic process management and measurement.

However, your systems implementations will only be as good as your process design. A computer system implementation is not a business process implementation, a computer system is a process tool, not the process itself, whatever the vendor says.

Design the process first, do not be swayed by a potential computer application. Competitive advantage and excellence comes from your organisation doing what you do better than anyone else—not by doing the same as everyone else.

Before proceeding, we need to have an understanding of the capabilities of BPMS. This is a business management book so is not about the technical aspects of computer systems, our concern is the functionality that computer systems bring to business processes.

Here are some of the features of all BPMS. Some BPMS and iBMS have additional features but these are the ones that can be taken into account in any SYSTEM design that assumes use of a BPMS.

Graphical workflow representation

BPMS use graphical process modelers to assist process and procedure design. These may accept input from diagramming tools such as Visio.

Web browser interface

The familiar web browser is used for user windows, although window content may be specific to the BPMS.

User windows

Each user may see different windows according to their roles, access permissions and the immediate task information requirements. Only relevant information is presented.

Moving tasks proactively

As soon as a task is complete the system notifies by email the person who is to do the next task that it is ready for them to work on and puts the task into their personal inbox. The notification email provides a hotlink to the inbox. There is no human effort required, there is no waiting time and people cannot delay the process on purpose.

Workflow inbox

The workflow inbox lists all tasks that are waiting for a performer to work on. It is automatically updated as tasks are completed or received.

Parallelism

Instead of activities being conducted sequentially or with only simple use of concurrent activities, a BPMS allows unlimited parallel streams of activities. This allows the introduction of ASAP thinking by branching from a critical event out into all tasks that can be conducted in parallel because they are not dependent on each other.

Conditions

Workflow can branch (take more than one direction, or pick one of alternate directions) depending on particular circumstances. The conditions for branching are configured into the BPMS and are triggered automatically by the system as the work progresses.

Time limits

The BPMS can be configured to know time limits for tasks and the action to be taken if they are exceeded.

Time can be specified as relative, for example, 2 days after completion of previous task, or absolute, such as on the first of every month.

Escalation and rerouting

Computerisation enables the system to be instructed as to what to do automatically if an activity is not completed in its allotted time or duration. The system can remind the performer before the time expires, escalate the matter if not completed on time, or reroute the task to someone else.

Routing to recipient

The system routes communications to the correct addressees. These emails are written as part of the system configuration and automatically sent as the workflow dictates. Addressees are identified personally, so the system needs to know who is performing a process role.

Roles

In order for the system to know who to send an email to it requires access to a database which it can use to match names to process roles. However, this may not be direct, the database may match process roles to job titles because the two are not the same, then the job title is connected to the person's name. The database can also include information on stand-ins who take on the role when the specified person is away, alternates to whom a task can be redirected if the task duration is exceeded, or overseers to whom the task is escalated if it is late.

The role database may be within the BPMS or be held outside of the BPMS and accessed as needed by the system.

Compiling the role database can be a significant undertaking and require communications to many stakeholders. It is also important to have mechanisms to keep the database up to date. Simple update processes can be used so that users maintain their own role information, rather than resorting to a centralised bureaucratic process.

Business rules

Business rules allow activities to be automated. A business rule is merely a machine-intelligible statement that examines input conditions and selects an appropriate decision without human intervention that is used to complete the activity. Automation speeds up processes greatly as there is no waiting time and work time is minimal. Moreover, the work time is 'free' (having acquired the hardware and configured software) because computers are not paid salaries.

Delay times

Parallel work streams started by branching will merge later on. The system can be instructed which (or all) of the tasks or activities immediately before the merge must be completed before moving to the next task or activity. Delay periods may be specified to implement time limits.

Dynamic forms

Processes typically use forms, but when using a BPMS, a form can be tailored according to the responses given by the user and so information that is not necessary for the instance being processed is not sought. This reduces effort filling in the form, avoids user frustration and speeds up the process.

Document attachment

Documents can be attached by users to the process records as the process advances.

Digital signatures

The system can accept the user sign-on as evidence that the person using the computer is whom they assert to be and so merely clicking on 'Yes', 'Accept' or a similar meaning button is deemed equivalent to a signature, hence 'digital signature'. This simplifies authorisations.

BPMN

Increasingly, modelers use Business Process Modeling Notation (BPMN) which is a set of icons for use in process models that clarify exactly what the user intends. Whilst BPMN is really useful for systems engineers it can be too complicated for business users that do not use it all the time. For this reason it is better used by the BPM

Specialist or a Business Analyst when documenting the first process draft and for updating thereafter rather than to originate the SYSTEM design. Moreover, to ensure business user comprehension only a limited set of BPMN symbols should be used which can be intuitively understood.

Once the business users are used to seeing BPMN models then it may prove acceptable to work on the business requirements using a BPMN modeler. The decision when to use a BPMN modeler is down to the BPM Specialist who must gauge what will work with the process team, but it is better not to force the issue so the tool gets in the way of process design.

Database connectivity

The system may access external databases. This may be for simple information storage or retrieval or it can be used to synchronise data across applications.

Integration and third-party applications

BPMS provide integration modules for major enterprise software applications that allow data and workflow to easily pass between applications. This saves a lot of customisation work that would otherwise have to be done.

Metrics

BPMS automatically collect metrics data regarding how processes are performing using the system.

Monitoring

Metrics data is rarely available for manual systems. BPMS enables the Process Manager to monitor process performance very easily and decide how the process can be improved.

Pitfalls developing business process computer systems

Workflow vs data perspective

The IT industry was driven by a data perspective for decades, the large IT vendors marketed database systems. These systems were essentially passive, they relied on the user to specify which function to call and use. The emergence of the process perspective in businesses caused a new demand for systems that moved work forward proactively, these became known as Business Process Management Systems (BPMS). The database vendors acquired emerging BPMS companies and developed their systems to incorporate BPMS functionality.

This may sound of little relevance today but some people in both business and the IT industry advanced their careers using database systems and still think that way—and have a database system set of assumptions and skills. Do not allow such people, who may be very clever and probably have good intentions, to select and implement a database system paradigm instead of a BPMS.

However, it is perfectly feasible to add a workflow system on top of existing database systems.

Using HTML

There is a further, probably more dangerous, technology trap and it arises from the prevalence of internet technologies. Hyper Text Markup Language (HTML) and its derivatives are the main markup languages for creating web pages and systems that can be displayed in a web browser. Many systems engineers are expert at using HTML and love developing HTML-based process systems. Developing systems purely in HTML results in individual systems for each process with high costs of maintenance and considerable re-inventing of the wheel, because BPMS have all of the workflow functions that are needed. BPMS typically use browser interfaces, so use internet technologies, but they provide a common platform for all processes, and individual processes are configured within the BPMS. This dramatically reduces maintenance costs and increases development speed and consistency.

Do not fall into the trap of allowing individual processes to be fully developed in stand-alone HTML systems.

However, it may be appropriate to have subroutines developed in HTML if the BPMS does not have the required functionality, and having the BPMS call the HTML subroutine as required. For example, if a process includes an algorithm for policy interpretation this may require some dedicated programming because the BPMS business rules module is not up to the task.

IT application selection

It is not essential to use a BPMS to computerise workflow and automate processes. A range of IT applications can be used, from email through to iBPMS. The selection of the right technical application platform for business processes is a project to be included in any process program.

The choice may be dynamic, starting with a relatively economic IT application for the organisation to learn about BPM and prove the business case, moving onto more sophisticated IT applications that deliver more functionality as the organisation's BPM capability develops.

The selection of the BPM IT application is a business investment decision and the Program Owner has the responsibility for progressing the decision. This may cause consternation in the IT department as it will be seen as an IT decision, but selection of any IT application should be seen as a business decision with technical advice as input. However selecting hardware platforms is an IT decision with the business providing transaction volume information as input. Of course, there should be collaboration as the IT department manages the technical architecture and needs to ensure the BPMS has adequate support infrastructure.

Application support

One of the big questions that arises is who will configure and maintain the BPMS. Vendors may say that the process model can be developed and maintained by business users and the process model is automatically implemented by the BPMS operational modules. This is ideal but these are complicated applications and the skills and focus on detail by system engineers will improve the system implementation. In consequence, a collaborative effort is needed to optimise the system implementation.

IT system ownership

Experience suggests that the best computer systems come from teams in which business users and IT engineers collaborate. This applies the best collective knowledge and skills to the projects.

However the system belongs to the business owner, eventually this will be the Process Owner but during the project it will be the Project Owner and the day-to-day manager is the Project Leader.

Following this logic the budget for the IT System, its development and its support belongs with the business. If the system is cross-functional which business unit budget carries the cost? The choice is between the Program Owner's, the Process Owner's, the CEO's, some form of allocation, or the IT department. It will probably be the latter but this does not bestow system ownership on IT. Resolution of this issue could result in some conflict but the principles need to be clearly established by the Program Owner before it gets too late.

Automate how much?

How automated should a workflow be? It might be assumed that the larger the percentage of automated activities/tasks the better. But there may be good cause not to over-automate, particularly in the first online version of what has been a people intensive process.

People can be very reluctant to hand over decision making to a machine, they fear that the machine will make wrong decisions because it cannot see the nuances of a particular case or does not understand the politics or relationships involved. There are other reasons which relate to losing control and influence, people may feel that replacing their decision making with a machine denigrates their worth and purpose in life, that their loss of influence will reduce their importance to the organisation.

These issues must be taken seriously, they can cause the system to be rejected regardless of how good it is.

A good approach is to allow a decision to be made off-line if a significant number of decision-makers assert that the decision is too hard to automate because of human factors—but put a tight duration on the activity or task. This covers decisions that:

- Are in response to situations that have large numbers of potentially influencing variables
- Require offline consultation
- Require contact with external parties who do not have access to the system
- Require decisions that are just too difficult to automate
- Are a governance approval

It may be decided to leave some decisions for offline assessment in order to allow confidence in the system to build up before automating the decision in a later version.

Where there are confidence and even loss of status issues a good strategy is to start with 20% to 30% offline decisions and reduce this percentage by automation as confidence improves and people see that the system is making their lives easier. Users will start suggesting additional automation and will state the decision criteria to be used in the business rules.

CHAPTER 8

SYSTEM design — Computerising the TO BE

Now the TO BE is complete, the next activity is to consider a SYSTEM process design. Although we are not yet configuring an IT system, we are looking at how the use of computer systems can affect the business process design at the activity level.

The TO BE can be implemented without a new computer system but these days most processes are implemented in computer systems. The SYSTEM design modifies the TO BE to take account of the functionality of the BPMS or other application used to implement the process.

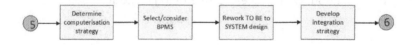

Computerisation strategy

If the computer application is already implemented in the organisation the constraints of the system may require modifications to the process. It is important to recognise the gap between the ideal situation and what can actually be computerised. Consideration can then be given to whether to accept changes to the process or whether to seek customisation of the application to allow the ideal process to be computerised. Customisation will result in higher maintenance costs so should not be undertaken lightly; at the same time, if the process needs to be changed to fit the system will the process be compromised?

The above concerns reflect constraints imposed by the system. There may also be opportunities that the functionality of the application offers for improvement of the TO BE design.

If a new BPMS is to be selected then completing a new process design first will improve the understanding of the team as to the functionality required of the new BPMS and improve the selection result.

If a BPMS has already been chosen, the TO BE design may be developed with the BPMS in mind and a separate SYSTEM design is unnecessary—the TO BE can incorporate the SYSTEM changes.

A strategy needs to be agreed for implementing the process on the chosen BPMS or application platform. The BPMS or other application will suggest how this is done in detail, but before that, it is necessary to be clear about what process level is being computerised.

Computerising workflow at the activity level

The simplest way to computerise workflow is at the activity level. This means implementing a workflow management system that routes work between people who complete tasks offline—or in other systems.

Assign a single responsibility for each business activity, even if work is done by other people, to—let's call them 'activity owners'—and specify flow between these activity owners. Each activity owner must complete their activity; the tasks are performed offline, although data input may be part of the activity. The owner can assign workflow system access rights to task performers who input the results of their tasks, but it is up to the owner to manage activity completion.

The simplest work routing technology is email with document attachments. This is not workflow management because the system is not proactive; each activity owner has to initiate an email with an attachment. A workflow management system would recognise completion of an activity, information is in the database ready for the next activity and the system emails the next activity owner with notice that a new task is in their inbox.

An activity workflow management system leaves task definition and task instructions to the activity owners. Work is decentralised to the area with best knowledge and skills, there is no attempt to specify work instructions in the system; however, data fields and document formats may be established to input or access activity information.

The advantage of activity workflow management is that it is process oriented rather than functionally oriented. Activity owners may assign tasks to people in different functions, or the organisation structure may change to group people with skills from different functions into activity teams. A low budget workflow management system may be a good first step towards learning about workflow management with an expectation of upgrading the system to BPM at a later stage.

Activity workflow management will result in significant reductions in wait times and overall process cycle time by agreeing activity durations and using rerouting, delegation, reminders and escalations to ensure the agreed durations are not exceeded. Typically, agreed durations are about the median time previously achieved, or a bit better, but the instances that previously did not meet median times will be much improved, lowering the new median. However, this strategy will not produce the work time and wait time elimination savings that can be achieved with automation using a BPMS.

Nevertheless, if the objective is to improve service to customers, this approach can be very effective. If the level of work requires mostly offline human interaction and there is little scope for automation then this is an appropriate approach. However, be wary that what could be happening is that inefficient people are mounting a rear-guard action to prevent others finding out what they do, or just do not want to discuss methods with outsiders.

It is surprising what can be achieved with this approach and it reduces the considerable amount of project work required to complete full business requirements at the task level for a BPMS.

Computerising at the task level, with automation

The above section described a simple computerisation of the workflow at the activity level. However, computer systems are typically implemented at the task level. BPM tracks tasks rather than activities and so includes business procedural instructions ('how' and 'who' rather than 'what' and 'when'). Procedure provides detailed information and routes workflow between performers according to their process roles.

To computerise at the task level requires completion of IT business requirements. But before diving into business requirements it is worth looking at the impact of information technology and discussing the appropriate technology strategy.

'Computerise' means to use computers to manage work, and includes 'Automate' which means to have computers actually do work instead of people doing it. The section above about computerising at the activity level was about computerising, not automating. The two words are often used synonymously but they in fact have different meanings.

Rework TO BE to SYSTEM design

The SYSTEM design is kept at the activity level, it is not developed as the procedure or business requirements workflow, even if the strategy is to implement at the task level. The purpose of the SYSTEM design is to work out how to further innovate the process leveraging technology.

The IT Manager should join the team to lend his/her technical knowledge to the proceedings and will preferably remain in the team right through to implementation. The expanded team uses the same workshop techniques used for the TO BE to progress the SYSTEM design.

The SYSTEM design may merely change the graphical representation of some activity boxes to denote that the activity is automated using business rules, but the design itself may change due to the capabilities of the BPMS, for example, increasing the numbers of activities done in parallel. It is not necessary to add activities for new flows such as escalation or rerouting as these are additional tasks for existing activities.

The SYSTEM design is helpful in specifying the activity level in a form better suited for the development of the business requirements; indeed, this may be the right time to switch from using simple charting tools for documentation of the workflow to using a BPMS modelling tool that can specify the process at the activity level. This will make it easier to drill down to the task level when working on the business requirements.

Develop Integration Strategy

The SYSTEM design may also consider data and information flows and integration with other databases and with other applications. This topic will be progressed in Chapter 10 – Application Development but preliminary discussion of the integration strategy is helpful once the computerisation strategy has been set and the BPMS or other application platform selected because the SYSTEM design may be impacted.

CHAPTER 9

Business Requirements — Detailing the Procedure, Specifying the System

Business requirements detail processes for development of online systems. Procedures add 'how to' and 'who' instructions to processes at the task level. In practice, the procedure is the business requirements that IT developers implement in the online system, because a separate procedure document is not required when all procedural instructions are included in context-sensitive help within the workflow system. Business requirements may include detailed flowcharts showing tasks unless the workflow is just computerised at the activity level.

Requirements may be developed by IT business analysts, BPM consultants or business users—or best of all, a combination of all of these as a project team.

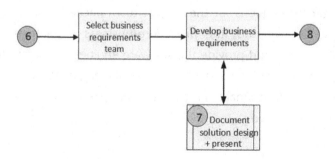

Developing the business requirements may take more time than previous phases put together because of the detail that has to be teased out, all of the screen and email wordings that need to be specified, and because, for automation, the business rules that are needed are in effect micro policy and may require time-consuming discussion and approval.

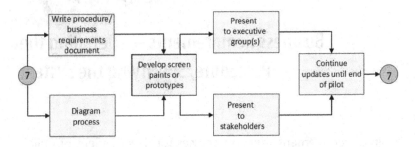

Write procedure/business requirements document

Conventionally, Business Analysts take the TO BE design and write business requirements for use by the software engineers, interviewing users as they go. Experience suggests that the engineers will make assumptions about what works best as they develop the system and sometimes this is not the way business users would prefer, had they thought about it. It is not the analyst's fault, the business users have surrendered detailed design to the analyst.

A better technique is for the project team (including a business analyst) to work out the procedure/business requirements in detail together and provide the software engineers with business requirements which are specific and leave the engineers to focus on the technical functionality of the system, which for a good system, can be complicated.

An option is to write the business requirements document and input the TO BE or SYSTEM workflow diagram at activity level straight into the BPMS. Many BPMS model processes at this level but the task level information still needs to be provided in a document. It is best to model the workflow at the task level in order to assure the logic in the document works.

Diagram process

The workflow at the task level requires many more boxes and arrows and responsibility information, 'Who', needs to be added, either in boxes, by colour coding, or by separating tasks into 'swim lanes'. The team evolves the detailed flowchart and documentation in parallel.

Develop screen paints or prototypes

Screen paints (pictures of how a computer screen will look without any workings behind it) or a prototype system (which demonstrate first draft workings as well as how screens will look) are very desirable whilst writing the business requirements. Users always have suggestions to make when they see what will appear on the screen which can avoid much later rework or a less than satisfactory final system.

After each workshop, the IT person works up screens in response to what requirements have been specified and brings them to the next workshop. This will usually result in some changes. The screen pictures become the primary documents upon which discussions are centred, but it is important to keep the business requirements documentation and workflow charts up to date with changes.

Present to executive groups

Completion of the business requirements, including documentation and screen designs, signifies the completion of the business aspect of solution design. Before showing the business solution to stakeholders the Program Team should check it within the business context.

The Program Owner or Manager will present the result to the Stakeholder Management Group (SMG) and the Executive Management Group (EMG), as governance and consultation activities. This has the additional advantage of ensuring the continued support of these groups.

These are not in-depth process briefings, rather a progress report on the fit of the TO BE with the following aspects of the business model.

Business Strategy

Does the TO BE implement the business strategy for which the program was initiated?

Business benefits

When implemented, will the TO BE enable the realisation of those business benefits?

Policies

Defining a process specifies how a policy is being implemented in detail. Policies, like laws, are subject to interpretation. Policies will be interpreted in defining a process—the program team needs to check whether policies will be adhered to and raise any ambiguities or conflicts.

Innovating a process may suggest that a policy needs amending. In this case, a policy amendment needs to be initiated.

Policy is usually the responsibility of an organisation's Board of Directors. The EMG will be briefed and take the policy issues to the Board.

Customer value

Will the TO BE deliver the right value to the customer? The meeting will tend to focus on organisational value of the TO BE but it is important that the executives responsible for customer relationships and service delivery agree with the anticipated customer value.

Goals

The corporate and program goals will have been included in the program terms of reference. The program team needs to refer back and document how those goals will be achieved by the TO BE.

Fit (process architecture)

The program team will show the fit of the TO BE process into the process architecture, to explain the process context and dependencies.

Synergies

The EMG and SMG will need to be aware of any synergies with other programs and if they have not been linked together, ensure that they are.

Constraints and opportunities

Time, resources, finances, competing programs, customer's needs, regulations, competitive activity, etc. can all cause constraints on the program and can sometimes provide unexpected opportunities. These need to be recognised and any program changes approved.

Dynamic impact

Once the TO BE has been completed a better understanding of the dynamic impact of its implementation can be assessed. Presenting this to the SMG and EMG provides advanced warning and enables preparation, or probably more accurately conditioning, to be commenced. This is probably a key communications milestone and the program team needs to have a communication ready for sign-off and issue by the Program Owner or CEO.

Present process to stakeholders

After the completion of the business requirements it is politic to present the complete procedural design to the executive management and stakeholders as screen paints or a prototype system.

Send an email after the meeting as a follow-up to allow for people to give feedback after they have thought about what they heard and discussed it amongst themselves. If serious issues are raised, talk to the stakeholders concerned face-to-face.

Update for feedback

After receiving feedback, the team meets and goes through the comments and suggestions. If ideas are rejected, be sure to note the reasons but whatever happens, respond to stakeholders stating what decisions have been made. This may be done by email, telephone or in person. Any ideas that are accepted will be entered in a change log and then implemented.

The updating activities continue right through to the end of the pilot, but it is best to publish new versions periodically that incorporate a list of updates rather than implementing updates individually.

Process procedural design principles and techniques

The following areas of design focus can lead to major design innovation and improvement.

Dwell time

Elimination of excessive dwell time (refer to chapter 6) delivers considerable value to customers at no additional cost to the organisation. It can deliver an enormous benefit to the organisation in terms of reputation, which generates new business and customer loyalty, ensuring repeat business. For public sector organisations it can result in a fundamental change of view by customers—from one of seeing the organisation as bureaucratic and difficult to deal with to one of recognising good customer service and valuing the support the organisation provides.

As business requirements are developed, maximum task dwell times are determined that balance improved process cycle time with reasonable times for people to manage their queue of work. Any task that is not completed within the maximum dwell time, after reminders, will be escalated or rerouted.

There will always be certain individuals who take too long to complete a task, sometimes because of their sense of self-importance but sometimes because they are just not well organised or have developed bad work habits. New process systems are a threat to them as their habitual practice of slow reaction time is exposed if escalation occurs. Their superiors will soon tire of receiving escalations and request improved performance. If performance does not improve then the person's recalcitrance is either suffered; their performance improves; they leave muttering that the organisation is not the same, it is going to the dogs, and they will not put up with the change; or the person is performance managed out of the organisation.

Micro policies

Computer systems run on 0 or 1, that is, absolute values without the use of human fuzzy logic and without the ability to consider nuances that humans perceive when making decisions. Humans tend to make a decision over and over again as it is presented to them each time. The path a particular instance takes through a process is decided by business rules which are specified during the business requirements phase, there is no repetition of the thought process. Accordingly, business rules have to be very clearly defined without any possibility of the system not knowing what to do, whatever the input information.

Business rules are in effect micro policy, they are the transactional interpretations of high level policy statements, implementing pre-specified decisions. When new systems are being designed, policy issues arise because policy is being interpreted and fixed at an operational level. There needs to be an established process for resolving policy issues that meets the governance requirements of the organisation without unduly holding up the progress of the project. The Program Owner has the responsibility for ensuring there is such a process and may have delegated authority to make micro policy decisions or be the person that takes the issue to the decision-making governance group.

Business rules

The business rules control the workflow so that policy and procedure are correctly implemented by the system. Each automated activity or task will have a business rule. The form a business rule takes is:

Input information > Condition question(s) > Rule > Output (action(s) or new condition)

The input information has been collected by the system up until this point. The condition question reviews the information and applying the rule determines the answer to the question, which becomes the output. Completion of the output is the trigger for the next task, activity or input information for the next business rule.

A succession of rules may be needed to complete an activity. If the rule is written at task level there will only be one question. IT people and BPMS write business rules at task level; however, it is open to business users to specify business rules at an activity level which will probably result in a succession of questions. The reason for writing business rules at the activity level is that the outcome from the activity is assured in business terms, which best correlates with the TO BE/ SYSTEM process design.

Here is an example of a rule written at activity level so that there is more than one question, the activity is 'Source furniture [for new employee]' (C4 is the activity reference):

Activity	Input information	Condition questions	Rule	Output
Source Furniture C4	Furniture stock quantities and costs Furniture specified according to grades Swappable furniture stock references by standard furniture references Furniture budgets by grade Approver for over budget situations	Is there furniture in stock of the required grade? Is there alternative furniture? Is alternative furniture within budget + 10%?	IF there is stock of required grade allocate the furniture IF there is no stock of required grade consider swapping alternative furniture; IF there is swappable stock check whether within budget + 10%, IF not in budget + 10 % email for approval; IF approved allocate stock, IF not approved order furniture; ELSE (there is no acceptable stock) order furniture	Furniture allocation OR action to order furniture. Instance Manager advice. Approval if cost of alternative furniture more than budget + 10%

The rule is written in plain English, but logical operators are used (IF and ELSE in this case, but others such as AND, OR, NOT, WHEN, THEN, can be used). Whilst logical operators are mostly used in computer programming languages they are also used in philosophy and indeed in everyday speech. The business rules written by business users are not intended to be programming statements, merely logical statements.

Business users may not need to specify input information or output, these can be determined by the IT people; what is critical for business users is that the rules are written to correctly implement policy and intended procedure. However, if business users are tracking information flows, which is recommended, then input and output columns are needed.

Note the use of ELSE above as a catch-all so the system will not hang if an unforeseen condition arises.

Business users need only write business rules for trickier activity level decisions, such as the above. The BPMS will implement them as successive single rules by task.

Simple business rules can be clearly indicated by decisions noted on alternate arrows leaving a task or activity box or flows may be from a decision gateway diamond symbol that states the condition question that is asked, rather from a box (see 'branching' below and diagram in screen paints later in the chapter).

Multiple paths

Online systems can manage multiple simultaneous tasks and workflows that dramatically reduce overall cycle time. They can also manage alternative workflow routes dependent upon the particulars of the instance being processed. This flexibility of processing is essential for an efficient and responsive organisation that caters for customers' individual requirements.

Fast track

Process flow can be simplified in some cases by identifying that not all activities or tasks need to be completed, probably because the particular case is straightforward. Another way of saying this is that more difficult cases should have exceptional activities or tasks handled in conditional branches (where the workflow splits into multiple paths) off the main process flow.

Another good way of fast tracking the majority of instances, particularly with the first version of new processes and systems, is to provide conditional branching for offline decision making when the case is tricky or unusual, simplifying the core process. This is a good strategy for gaining acceptance of new processes or systems as users feel they still manage the more difficult cases, and it enables quicker implementation of the core process.

Over time, users suggest more and more conditions that can be automated with new business rules and branching, reducing the number of decisions they need to make and therefore their workload.

Branching

Every branching in a workflow has a business rule. For simple rules the rule can be written on the workflow diagram arrows, the direction of the output arrow implements the decision.

Be careful when writing arrow statements that they clearly indicate whether all branches are to be followed (parallel, no conditions on arrows indicates this sort of branching and flow), all conditions are to be evaluated and those that are true followed (inclusive, usually each flow statement starts with 'If') or only one of the alternatives (exclusive, only one If statement can be met, to the exclusion of other If statements) is to be followed. If the arrow statements are not clear flow may be ambiguous and incorrectly implemented. BPMN, as explained next, offers gateway symbols that are explicit.

Business workflow diagrams need to be readily understood by business users who do not work on systems all the time. The IT industry, catering for analysts who work on systems all the time, has developed a diagramming symbol set called Business Process Modelling Notation (BPMN) which provides extended symbolised information which tends to be too much for business users and detracts from the focus of user workshops. Whilst boxes and arrows are the basic components of workflow diagrams, a few of the BPMN symbol set[xviii] can be used to clarify meaning.

Configuration of a BPMS will require a business rule be put into the system for every branch, but if the modelling is done in the BPMS modelling module using BPMN symbols, the BPMS may interpret the business rule from the business requirements workflow diagram. If business rules are written directly into a BPMS, they will be at task level and will take a form specified by the BPMS.

Workflow diagrams examples are shown later in this chapter.

Approvals and sign-offs

Governance requires approvals to ensure policies are implemented and to monitor strategic performance, or to prevent breach of policies before they occur. However, the responsibility for operational performance should be with the performer, the manager's responsibility is to ensure skills, competence, tools and information are in place before the activity occurs; therefore, approvals should not be used as a device to check performance. Monitoring can be achieved by other observational or measurement techniques.

Sign-offs are different to approvals, they may be required to document commitment to a plan or action, and are part of governance processes. In some cases a large number of sign-offs are required for a large complex plan, but the sign-offs do not represent approval of the plan, only the signatories' commitment to achieve their part of the plan.

Managers with a responsibility for a particular service do not need to sign off to show commitment to perform what is their normal responsibility. Sign-offs are only required to show commitment to unique or non-conforming plans or actions.

Reduction in the number of approvals and sign-offs in a process is a good way of reducing delays and improving cycle time. If a senior person has approved a plan and functional managers have been advised, there is no need for them to approve as well. Removal of approvals can be a very emotive issue, managers may not like losing their approvals as they see it as a loss of status. Leadership on the issue is required to prevent attempts to undermine the adoption of the new process, and the objective of improved customer value through reduced lead times must be made paramount.

Rerouting and escalation

Modern BPMS enable every activity to have a maximum duration time, which if exceeded, triggers a rerouting of the activity or escalation to prompt action by a more senior person. An example of this is a service fault escalation process, the first level of support (routine, low technical knowledge, short amount of time allowed to fix the problem) has a set time before the fault is escalated to level 2 support (technical product/service knowledge but not experts) and if they do not solve it after a further pre-defined time, the fault is escalated to level 3 (high technical competence level). In a bureaucratic organisation the time allowed may be days but the principle remains the same.

Escalation can become an emotional issue for people who routinely hold up actions as this pattern becomes obvious. Previously, everyone down the chain just had to wait and it was accepted as normal. There might have been the odd complaint but likely the offender would claim they were under pressure from their workload and probably nothing changed for more than a week or two. However, when the process adds to the superior's workload they tend to call the offender to account.

Performers quickly learn to complete an activity as soon as possible rather than as late as possible or they find that support from their manager wanes and ultimately they may be told to change or leave. Occasionally someone cannot change and they become resentful at being continually chased and shown up and become so uncomfortable that they leave of their own accord.

Front-loading

The more that necessary information can be collected early in the process, the less the delay later in the process and the less the number of times the system has to be accessed. With a manual system, or even some database systems, people tend to provide only the information for the current task, even when little effort is required to provide information for later use.

With a good process design, early information collection can be the norm by requiring the information to be completed before the system will move to the next task. However, override needs to be allowed in case information is not yet available in the particular instance so as to avoid unnecessary delay. If this occurs, the system needs to set a condition flag and run the outstanding data collection task in parallel until the missing information is collected later on.

Moreover, when designing the process, being aware that information is available earlier than for the AS IS may suggest an improved sequence of tasks, improving efficiency.

Format

Even when using a BPMS, the screen background design needs to be consistent with corporate publication style guides and Marketing may need to be involved in designing the screen background.

At the same time, the process needs an identity of its own to aid marketing the new process and system later on. This will add project or program icons and tag lines to the screen background design.

The program as a whole also needs a format guide, covering consistent use of buttons, input fields, pop-up help, messaging, etc. so that users can readily use different processes because commands and style are consistent.

The key is to make screens user friendly and intuitive. Screens must not be cluttered and they need to complete one task or activity at a time.

A scrolling screen may be used if there is a sequence of connected tasks within an activity or for a smart form, but it still needs to close at a point when a user has completed the task or activity.

It is worth saying that a lot of IT people are expert system developers but if they are expected to do screen design may not come up with the best result, a specialist graphic designer is needed as they have that particular skill. The program team should ensure access to a graphic designer or a communications specialist not just for system screen layouts but also for program websites and communications.

Another tip is that developers may complete a function and just clear the screen. Users panic if the screen clears and they do not know if the system has accepted their input, so a screen message indicating acceptance before clearing the screen or moving to the next screen is needed. The principle is for the system to communicate clearly with the user.

Catch-all

There is nothing more frustrating for a user than a system hanging. With workflow, the danger is that the system encounters a condition which has not been pre-specified so it does not know what to do. As it is not possible to anticipate all situations, use of a catch-all is common practice. Specify for known situations then state what the system should do if none of these conditions apply. There must be no dead-ends unless the process is complete or is being exited.

Catch-alls are primarily implemented when specifying the business rules, basically they say 'if all of the above conditions do not apply then ...'. The logical operator that means this is 'ELSE'.

Process metrics and reporting

BPMS are really good at collecting process metrics in a way that manual systems cannot and for which other systems are less proficient. The purpose is to measure processes to show problem activities and performers, but at a higher level the process cycle times and other metrics will prove the value of the new process and system and therefore the value of the process program.

Although instance or case content may affect durations, measure overall process performance rather than case performance using Key Performance Indicators (KPI).

Process metrics and reporting are reviewed by the process manager and owner for possible process improvement opportunities.

Process KPI Examples[xix]

- Cycle time
- Work (resource consumption) time or cost
- Customer satisfaction
- Staff satisfaction
- Quantity of transactions per (time period)
- Transaction capacity per (time period)
- Error, complaint or rework volumes or costs
- Competitive score
- Quantity of process handoffs
- Industry specific measures

Organisation and method

Teaming

Business requirements for the IT system are best developed by the project team with business users and IT developers working collaboratively, led by the project leader who is a business manager. This ensures that whilst the business drives specification, technical opportunities and constraints are dealt with as they arise. It also enables the developers to generate screen-based feedback for the team quickly; seeing a system on screen as opposed to as a verbal description, even a flowchart, always provides 'aha' moments that lead to improved design and reduced rework later on.

This compares with a common approach whereby the IT team takes the TO BE, adds a functional requirements document asking business users clarifying questions as they go, then has the business manager sign off the 'business requirements' as the base document for system development. The IT team then develops a system away from the users. This shifts the onus of developing some of the fine detail procedural assumptions onto the IT analysts whereas they should remain with the business users. The result is a sub-optimised system and more rework.

Documentation

Assuming a collaborative approach, business requirements documentation can be actually written by a BPM Consultant, a Business Analyst or a competent business user. Sometimes if the project leader is the ultimate beneficiary of the system he/she will write the business requirements document, leaving diagrams to others. Diagrams can be done on screen in workshops using a diagramming tool such as Visio or a BPMS modelling tool, or on a white board in the workshop with fair copy documentation between workshop sessions using the same tool options—or a combination of both techniques. Similarly, the business requirements document can be developed on screen using a word processor or the project leader may prefer to develop a draft offline and bring printed copies to the team meeting for comment and improvement.

Screen paints

The IT analyst or graphic designer develops screen paints (what the system will look like on screen once developed, but without any workings) or prototypes (screens with workings, but not the final system) which are shown at the workshops as soon as possible. Seeing the system on screen for the first time always leads to improvements.

Freezing requirements

The business requirements are frozen ready for configuration of the BPMS or system development when the team considers that all improvements they can imagine for this version have been incorporated. Alternatively, if a time box/agile approach is used requirements are frozen when a predetermined cut-off point is reached.

The requirements may be updated later for changes through trial and pilot.

IT project culture risks

If business users allow IT to run the process project they open themselves up to some serious risks. They are not IT's fault—IT relates to how it has traditionally done work, so it is up to business users to manage these risks.

IT projects have tight deadlines, the pressure is on. There is a danger of seeing the process innovation stage as too difficult, better to computerise some version of current practice with some tweaks in order to get something out there. This is a common failing of IT-driven process projects because the system is seen as the deliverable. This is an illusion. Better to spend time up front getting the process and business requirements right so that time will be saved downstream as the number of iterations and versions will reduce and the system will do what is best for the business.

IT has established methodologies, including consulting users (good), and picking the best of the alternative current practices (seems good but is not). The objective for a new system is to devise a new method that is *better than all current practices*, which all users can buy into. Do not expect an IT-based business analyst to do this for you, the business people have to work it out in process projects.

Unless convinced about BPMS, IT people tend to favour database-based systems, this is what they have worked on for a long time. Database systems are reactive; they are driven by the assumption of adding, editing or deleting data. To do this, the user picks which screen to use to maintain the database. So, database systems have 'functions' that are called by the user. You will see flowcharts in the business requirements for database systems, but these are just for functions. On the other hand, workflow managers or BPMS are proactive, they implement processes not just functions, *and work is proactively presented to the user by the system.* This approach is fundamentally different and not natural to many IT developers. Beware, if you let IT drive the process project you will probably get a database system. This is no disrespect to my IT friends; they are clever and do a good job … according to their training. It is up to the business leaders to own and drive process system projects.

Additional Tools

In addition to workflow charts, two types of document can be used for procedure/business requirements.

Activity profile

The Activity Profile is useful for expanding information about the TO BE or SYSTEM design and may be used as a first stage towards a procedural or business requirements document. An example is shown in Appendix G. The information is in business language, not technical language.

If a prototype or screen paint set is being developed at the same time as the development of business requirements, then Activity Profiles may be adequate documentation with screen prints, instead of the full Procedure/Business Requirements Document below.

Procedure/business requirements document

The team develops a document that describes the procedure for the process at task level, that is, specifying what work is done by whom and how it is done in detail. This means taking the business activities that have already been specified and drilling down to the next level. The document tells the story of the process, how it progresses, what information is brought up and displayed and what information is gathered and how it is processed. It will describe what words are to be used on screen, what help information is to be accessible, and the access rights (which users can see what information).

This is a painstaking, iterative and time-consuming effort that needs to be correct in order for the IT developers to develop the right system without substantial rework.

The words to appear on screen, in pop-up help and in emails are specified in this document so that the developers can use correct phraseology from the beginning. The alternative is that if software engineers develop the system from the activity level TO BE/SYSTEM, without a detailed business requirements document, the team will need to improve the wording as engineers' language tends to be too terse and business users need greater clarity

Task level flow chart

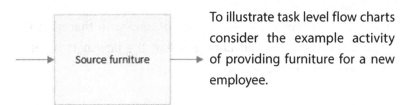

To illustrate task level flow charts consider the example activity of providing furniture for a new employee.

The procedure for completing the activity is quite complicated as alternative ways of completing the requirement are allowed for; the tasks are:

- Determine the appropriate furniture for the employee's grade.

- Check stock availability.
- If the right furniture is not available, considering swapping furniture that is available elsewhere.
- Failing which, consider different furniture that is available in stock.
- And if this is the case, and it is more expensive than the furniture for the new employee's grade +10%, get approval.
- Impact on budget requires approval.
- And if none of this works, order new furniture.
- And advise the instance manager of the result.

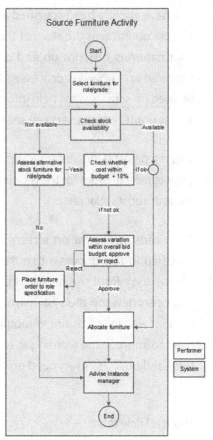

The flowchart (right) has been drawn using a simple diagramming tool, similar to that used for mapping activities. The advantage is that the flowchart is easily understood by business users.

However, the IT industry has developed a workflow symbol set called Business Process Model and Notation (BPMN). The advantage of using BPMN is that maps can be drawn using the modelling modules in BPMS and so provide information directly to the BPMS for system configuration. This reduces the IT development work load and speeds up development time.

In practice, by the time business users have reached the business requirements stage, even if this is their first process project, they have learned enough about flowcharting and process definitions to be able to come up to speed with BPMN quite quickly—so BPMN may be the preferred method for detailing business requirements workflow. However, it is best to use a simple BPMN symbol set rather than using the whole set, as some symbols are quite obscure to business users. The IT people can always add or substitute such symbols before submitting the model to the configuration input processes of the BPMS.

Below is the source furniture example diagrammed using BPMN, using a restricted BPMN symbol set.

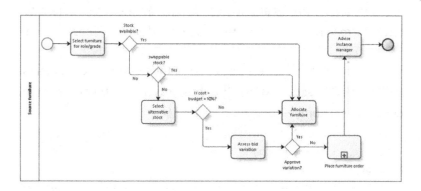

The diagram has been drawn using a popular BPMS modelling tool.[xx] Every diamond represents a question to be answered according to information already in the system and depending upon the answer, the business rule will tell the system what to do. In the diagram this result is represented by the branching in the flow with the answer to the question beside the arrows.

The box with a '+' at the bottom means there is a workflow elsewhere detailing the tasks, so this box in an activity or a subprocess, not a task.

The full BPMN symbol set is available online.[xxi]

Screen paints

The IT analyst or graphic designer develops screen paints (what the system will look like on screen once developed, but without any workings behind the screens) or prototypes (screens with workings, but not the final system) which are shown at the business requirements workshops as soon as possible. Seeing the system on screen for the first time always brings about ideas for improvement, which lead to further screen paints until the team is satisfied with the presentation.

The screen paints are an essential part of the business requirements and must be accepted by the business users before system development commences.

Matrices

Activity matrices have been referred to previously (AS IS Process Matrices). The rows (activities) will need updating to the TO BE design then additional information can be added to during the business requirements phase, for example in the matrix below three new columns have been added:

Process:				User:			Version	Date	
......	Resp.	Techniques/ tools/ docs	Completion condition	Output/ deliverable	Successor	Screen	Business Rules	Form

Business rules matrix

Business rules can be directly written in a matrix that refers to the activity or task, refer to the matrix for 'Source Furniture' example cited previously (p166).

Emails matrix

Workflow systems generate a lot of emails because the system is driving the process. These emails need to be written by business users for incorporation into the system configuration. There is a tendency to leave email drafting 'until later' and stop-gap abbreviated emails get incorporated into the system. Users find these obscure and the new process falls into disrepute. Write the emails as the business requirements evolve.

Here is an example matrix for the furniture example:

Ref	Content	Addressee(s)	Trigger	Header	E-mail subject matter text
C4-1	Alternative stock furniture approval request	COO	No stock AND alternative in stock AND alternative cost > bid cost + 10%	XYZ	'Below is an alternative furniture list available in stock but at a higher cost of $[.........] compared with the bid cost of $ [............]. Please approve or reject, in which case standard furniture will be ordered.'
C4-2	Alternative > cost furniture approved	FACMAN	COO approves /rejects alternative stocked, higher cost furniture	XYZ	'The COO has approved the alternative furniture list.' OR 'The COO has rejected the alternative furniture list, please order new furniture to specification'

C4-3	Advise instance manager of furniture source	PACMAN	Furniture sourced	XYZ	'Furniture has been sourced [from stock] [from stock to a higher specification (call FACMAN for more information)][by ordering new furniture, ETA [/ /]]'

Reports matrix

Report format requirements are often specified by drawing empty reports. Another technique is to use a matrix, for example:

Ref	Content	Available to	Availability	Header	Columns (character width) (total)
C4-1	Furniture source report	FACMAN, COO	Any time. On screen and print.	Furniture sourcing20xx	Bid no. (5), bid name (20), client (20), furniture amount $'000s (5), source (12), supplier (12), order date (8), floor location (8), user name (12), manager (12) comments (34)(136)

Data models

Often, business users leave information flows and data modelling to the IT people. However, it is a good idea for business users to at least understand the data model (which plots all information used by the process and the relationships between data) although they will most likely rely on an IT analyst to develop the data model. Understanding the data model can lead to insights into how and when to collect information during the process and when multiple processes are being developed, a pan-process data model is essential to understand how to source and reuse data across different processes.

Refer to Wikipedia[xxii] for more information on data modelling.

Data and information diagrams

How the information is collected and distributed is the subject of data and information diagrams. It is useful for business users to understand how information flows between tasks and activities and particularly between different processes; however, developing data and information flow diagrams can be tricky and is best left to trained IT analysts. The analyst can point out technical difficulties with the business requirements, particularly with regard to information gathering, and thereby prevent excessive development iterations.

CHAPTER **10**

Application Development — Building the System

This book is not intended to offer expert technical advice on BPMS or applications development. What follows is for business people who want to understand how to manage their side of the IT interface and ensure they get the system that implements the intended process.

For detailed IT technical work, readers need to consult technical specialists. Nevertheless, in order to have enough understanding there are some IT technical issues that need to be discussed.

Iterations

The frozen business requirements form the basis for the final system. However, it may have been developed progressively from the screen paints or directly in the BPMS as a prototype. Each version of the system as it grows is presented to the team and modifications are agreed so that shortly after the business requirements are frozen, the pilot system is ready for trial. This approach is practical using a BPMS, less so for a conventional customer built application.

The advantages are that the system is optimised from a business perspective and gets to pilot stage more quickly.

System configuration

Once the business requirements have been frozen, system configuration or application development can go into high gear. Even if a prototype is well advanced there will still be further work to be undertaken by the IT people before the system is ready for testing.

The final development time cycle should be quite short, typically a month for each process if a developer works on it full-time, to reach a system ready for stakeholder review.

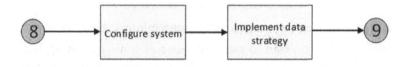

Systems integration

When introducing a process application into an organisation that has already invested in a number of IT systems, particularly large ones such as enterprise resource planning (ERP), customer relationship management (CRM), Finance, HR, and industry-specific operational management systems, the issue of integration across systems arises very quickly.

It is hard to hand off information mid-process between different applications, although there are applications that have been in use for many years called Enterprise Application Integration (EAI) applications that do this. EAIs map data for transfer between different applications that have different record structures. It is much easier if multiple processes are located on a single BPMS platform, in which case, activities can be maintained in a BPMS library and called by different processes.

This still leaves the issue of moving from existing enterprise systems to new process systems and vice versa.

The idea behind EAI is now incorporated in BPMS and modern BPMS provide a number of interfaces with widely used enterprise systems. However, issues of integration can slow down operationalisation of new processes. There is a data integration strategy that has advantages.

Integration using a process information database

New processes do not want to collect anew information that is already available, this can lead to inconsistencies as some data is updated but other supposed copies are not. Also, to copy information from one system to another is likely to result in transcription errors and excessive resource consumption. The integration functions in BPMS may be a solution but there is another approach.

The concept of using one source of data for all uses is called 'normalisation' or 'one source of truth'; however, the concept allows for collection of data in one place and propagating the data across other data locations so that all data is synchronised. This latter approach leads to an integration strategy which is particularly useful in process programs.

To integrate the new process with existing systems is technically time-consuming and creates additional points of error or failure which do not relate directly to the new workflow. It is much preferred to set up the new process stand-alone to prove the process and system before directly integrating it with other systems. This enables the new system to go to pilot quickly, even become fully operational if the process data can be maintained without writing to other databases without causing major issues.

The data is held in a process information database, this is distinct and separate from the BPMS database that contains process performance and tracking information.

Initially, the process information database can be populated from other sources, even manually for trials, and the new process system run stand-alone until it is proven and error-free. Once that is done, the process information database can be linked to other existing databases with periodic synchronisation and the systems become integrated and data is normalised, albeit not in real-time.

The goal is to set up the process database to source information from other systems and write data to other systems regularly, but not simultaneously, so as not to hinder the process workflow. This makes it easier to maintain systems in their own right and ensures rapid response time for users.

As more and more processes are set up, the processes become the source of data used by existing systems—reversing the information flow—thereby improving the efficiency of existing systems which no longer have to seek direct input. In fact, quite apart from a good way to develop new process systems this is a strategy for extending the life of existing, expensive, large systems.

BPMS and the technical architecture

IT engineers like to devise custom software, but it is expensive to maintain. For automating business processes a lot of the hard work has been done by the BPMS vendors. Pick the right BPMS (one that does not generate custom code) and configure it. You then use the BPMS for every process and are in a position to normalise data and reuse components ('services' or 'functions').

A major advantage of the data integration strategy is that it enables processes to be laid across existing database programs that do not have workflow, as is the case with many database systems (remember, the difference between a workflow system and a database system is that a workflow system moves work proactively whereas a database system relies on the user knowing which screen to call, so is passive).

This enables the new BPMS to be added to the technical application architecture as an additional layer above existing applications.

Testing

Before testing the system it is worth running a 'walkthrough' to ensure the process functionality works correctly. A walkthrough is simply a group of people (the team, or better, users) taking on roles and completing activities as set down in the process, either around a table or by email or using a dedicated program. Once the process is confirmed, the system can be tested.

Testing the new system should involve everyone.

- Business users test for functionality, usability and errors.
- IT people test for function, system integrity, database integrity and update/integration functions, platform loading and response time, scalability and maintainability.
- The process team tests for system accuracy of process, correct outcomes, and process performance or cycle time compared with existing processes.

Actual live data needs to be compiled to perform testing, that is, put through the system and observed for any of the above issues. Existing processes must of course continue to run as the new system is not yet operational. Do not use test results in operation.

The testing process is mapped below.

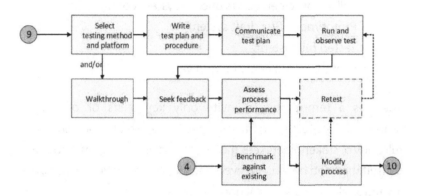

Look for ways to simplify process, and to develop early completion of activities or inputs. Estimate process times and durations. Formats do not have to be fully developed as the testing may reveal better ways of presenting information; however, the team should feel they are already serviceable.

It is essential that there are feedback mechanisms as part of testing, it may be face-to-face, by email or through a website or over the phone, but whatever the mechanism, there should be a log for recording all feedback and resultant action and to ensure feedback is provided. Above all, use good feedback, do not ignore it. Any issues arising are to be resolved and if necessary tests are rerun.

Do not go to pilot without running all of the tests

Stakeholder Reviews

As well as the main review points discussed earlier, there are additional stakeholder reviews that can be done during system development by inviting stakeholders to on-screen demonstrations.

- Full set of screen paints prior to system configuration
- Prototype or first draft system
- Tested full system
- Piloted system ready for go-live

There is a temptation to invite only key users or pilot user representatives to the first two or three of these but the earlier the full body of stakeholders sees the system that is coming the better the consultation and buy-in. Not everyone may come, but invite them, the invitation demonstrates willingness to listen.

The first two reviews are particularly good at picking up false assumptions made by the team with which stakeholders take issue. Conversely, objectors may be surprised at how good the new process looks and change their views. This is not unusual because until now they have been imagining what is coming and assuming the worst; however, if reviews have been done during the business solution phase objectors should be on-board by now.

Detractors may try and derail the project during and after reviews, more on this in the 'Implementing the Change' chapter, but be ready and stay calm. If most stakeholders buy in then detractors either come round or become strident and isolate themselves. Buying-in will occur if the process has been innovated to something clearly better. If the process has merely been improved then the territorial arguments may gain traction.

The final review is for intended users to see what will be coming to their desks shortly, the review is really part of user training but allows for some final feedback before go-live.

Documentation

Documentation should be completed as projects progress.

There is a risk that as IT develops prototypes and first versions of the system, the documentation of the business requirements falls behind as improvements are made directly to the system. Business requirements should be kept up to date so that the system documentation remains current for later use.

Once testing is complete, requirements will be frozen and any further ideas will be held over for a later version. The final business requirements documentation should reflect what is frozen. There will be bug fixes during the pilot and there may be improvements based on user feedback that really need to be incorporated into the go-live system that are accepted. Strict change control is required for these changes and business requirements documentation will need to be updated as the changes are implemented.

Before implementation planning commences, the team should review documentation and update and complete it as necessary. Presenting documentation to stakeholders may merely be a matter of publishing a website which stakeholders can go to once they have seen system demonstrations.

Organisations all have their own documentary requirements and the review should encompass these requirements.

Documentation and primary stakeholder reviews should be completed before commencement of the pilot and maintained during the pilot in readiness for implementation planning.

CHAPTER 11

Managing Change — Changing How People Do the Work

In this context 'change management' refers to how a new process and system is implemented and taken up by the performers and users. In order to plan and execute a good implementation plan it is necessary to have a good understanding of change management and to take the necessary actions from the beginning of the program to end up with a good implementation. Whilst change management is necessary in the design phase it is vital in the implementation phase.

Change Management

Change management is about dealing with people. It is not adequate to steam roller people into a change in today's world. Old-fashioned assumptions that people need to do what they are told to keep their jobs is not how to run an efficient organisation, it will merely get people to work and what they do thereafter will be much less than ideal due to the lack of commitment.

Change management principles and critical success factors (CSFs)

History provides lessons as to what principles make for a good change. The following critical success factors embody these principles and need to be met to ensure a successful implementation of any organisational change:

Sponsorship (Ownership)

Any change will fail if there is a lack of sponsorship, or ownership, objectors will move into the void and prevail. The sponsor needs to be well-regarded throughout the organisation and hold a senior role and have real influence. They must be willing to be the front person for the program, and be enthusiastic about the benefits of the program. It is up to the Program Owner to take on the role of sponsor or ensure that there is an effective, proactive sponsor who is a more senior person.

Involving stakeholders

Involving stakeholders brings understanding and reduced opposition—hopefully leading to commitment and active support. On the other hand, not involving stakeholders will certainly result in opposition as the stakeholders perceive they are being robbed of influence and are being put upon. This means more than having a stakeholder committee or group—which is essential—it means involving stakeholders in the workings of the program; in particular, involving stakeholder representatives in project teams, interviewing stakeholders and inviting stakeholders to progress reviews.

Identifying barriers and dealing with them

Identify detractors and approach them directly and early. Do not be tempted to put it off until later in the hope that others will persuade them to change their view, this is unlikely to happen and the detractors will become more entrenched in their views, attract adherents and mount effective opposition.

As well as dealing with detractors, there may be aspects of culture, custom and practice that militate against the program. These may be difficult to deal with and the unwavering support of the sponsor and other leaders is essential to convince people that a change is going to happen.

Some program and project managers try and push through resistance rather than engaging with the resistors, this will often result in increasing levels of resistance and lobbying of leaders until a point is reached at which leaders perceive a looming failure and move to close down the program or project.

It is essential to identify emerging barriers and deal with them. To get people to change their viewpoint takes effort on their part and will often result in them becoming vocal supporters once they have bought into the change.

Enquiry: asking instead of telling

In the early stages it is important to ask open questions and seek feedback. Advocating and selling do not come until the implementation phase before which the enquiring behavior will elicit objections and suggestions and dealing with them will minimise opposition.

Enquiry is the way to talk to detractors, find out why they have their opinions and discuss whether the grounds for their objections are valid in this particular case. This activity may well result in new ideas to accommodate their issues without distorting the program and discussing issues with them may result in their modifying their objections if they can see that their objections are being taken into account. To understand more about the psychology dealt with by enquiry, look up 'The Ladder of Inference'.[xxiii]

Dialogue initially: open discussion instead of advocacy

Taking enquiry further, dialogue is about putting aside opinions and convictions before going into a conversation, having an open mind. This is at the opposite end of the spectrum to advocacy, or selling your own conviction, which will become important once process and system designs are complete. Before this stage an objector who can see that you are offering to engage in dialogue is more likely to fall back from advocacy to negotiation, or even dialogue, and open up the possibility of a change of view leading to an accommodation.

Momentum

Momentum is required to demonstrate progress, this is not to advocate action at all costs, rather to keep things moving and not allow people's unavailability to slow momentum. Make it clear that workshops and reviews will occur as planned, if people are not available they can send a delegate once or twice, but not repeatedly.

Momentum is particularly important moving from implementation to operation. This is not just about project management discipline, it is about the behavior of systems. Any system is inherently stable; any current set of practices will resist change. In order to bring about change, the current system has to be destabilised and pushed into the new way of doing things. The change-over point from the old to the new way of doing things is the 'Tipping Point'[xxiv] and is unstable. Unstable situations may resolve by going back to the old way, which is more comfortable, rather than moving on to the new way. To achieve change, the time at the tipping point needs to minimised, and to achieve this, a sense of urgency is needed to keep up momentum.

Implementation planning

Tight, careful planning of a change implementation is required to maintain momentum. Typically, the roll-out and go-live of new processes and systems are planned day by day in detail so that everyone knows what is going to happen and to prevent missteps that might make the change falter.

To reduce risk and demonstrate operational benefits more quickly it may be decided to implement new processes and systems in phases, typically by subprocess. Each phase will require detailed implementation plans.

Communication

Communication is an extension of involvement. Communication is essential to allow people to come to terms with what is coming, to understand what it means to them, and to build up anticipation. It is best to use a professional communications specialist to draft and issue communications, they know the right language to use. Communication starts with an announcement from the sponsor of the program or project and identifies the participants. Over time, it reports on progress and the frequency of communication builds up as implementation approaches.

Feedback and response

Feedback should be encouraged and contact points clearly displayed in all communications. Feedback is a valuable source of information about issues and concerns. All feedback should be logged and acknowledged, with a statement as to what action will be taken or at what point any decision for action will be made. The reaction to feedback should be genuine and open, not dismissive or grudging. Feedback will often point to improvements that can be made quite simply.

Change management process

This is a generic change management process:

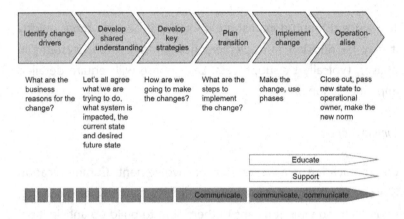

The diagram displays the need for involvement and communication, which are the key elements of change management. It requires accommodation of different views and listening skills. When the time comes for implementation, most of the objections need to have already been dealt with. Nevertheless, barriers do arise.

Organisational barriers to process innovation

Effective process change is only achieved if barriers are anticipated and removed before they can cause real damage to the program and projects.

People are control oriented, it is normal human behaviour. Loss of control is stressful and so any perception of a potential loss will have people up in arms, or at least worried. Here are some of the barriers to innovation:

Power, authority and status

Vested interests in status and existing power structures lend people authority within the organisation. Threatening the bases of authority and influence will provoke a strong response. Often the people involved have achieved their present level of power and influence because of their political skills, and these will have to be faced.

Investment

Individuals will have put their reputations on the line to ensure certain investments have been made by the organisation. Any attempt to diminish or render obsolete such investments may well provoke a response. A process program or project may appear to make some existing investments less important because their justification was based on functional efficiencies whereas we know from the Theory of Constraints that organisational efficiency needs to focus on constraint activities, which may not be in the function sponsoring the investment.

Commitment

People are committed to a particular paradigm, they believe that is how the world should be. Process organisation presents a new paradigm and people may reject it because it does not fit their worldview.

Uncertain future

Poorly understood change is stressful, loss of control over our lives is stressful. Uncertainty about the future will lead people to try and control change to preserve their current comfortable position.

Inertia

People get comfortable with how things are, they cannot be bothered with changing things, and it interferes with their routine.

Technical specialisation

Technical specialisation can remove an enterprise view. Careers are typically built on technical specialisation. What happens is that focus on a specialisation over many years removes the ability to see the wider picture. The enterprise view only really takes shape when a person joins a senior management team. Nevertheless, able demonstration of the wider picture may enable some to revise their viewpoint.

Protection of territory

Humans are naturally territorial; so protective behaviour of functional 'silos' and operational areas inevitably occurs. This is hard to circumvent because groups develop an insular, resistant view in the face of pressure to change. If this cannot be pre-empted by inoculation (see below), then the Sponsor needs to lead the way by making clear his/her expectations that a broader view will be adopted by all involved.

Personal responsibility

Culture often results in 'pass the parcel' behaviour. This arises because the enterprise is managed on a personal responsibility rather than a collaborative model. If personal responsibility is assumed to mean that each individual will be judged on how they complete their list of tasks, rather than how they contribute to processes, then an attitude prevails that responsibility stops when a task is completed and passed to the next person. Overcoming this culture is a key step in moving to a process-centric view, and again leadership is the key. This is not to remove personal responsibility, rather to remove the isolationist attitude that can come with it.

The internal customer

The 'internal customer' mental model arises when inward-facing departments or divisions are told they must focus on the customer. Their response can be that the next department in the value chain is their customer. When they are the larger and more influential department this enables the functional leader to dominate the conversation and specify what will be delivered by his/her department. It is essential that in process work the external customer is the only customer.

Some other terminology is needed for the internal customer, perhaps using the word 'next' to denote connectedness, for example, 'next performer' or 'next value-add contributor', abbreviated to 'next value-add' or 'next contributor'.

Complex politics

In hierarchical organisations the political tactics between functional heads can become complex and very difficult for a CEO to deal with. The CEO wants to keep all of his/her reports onside and tends to try and deal with the heads individually. What is needed is to deal with the functional heads collectively, driving the higher ideal of subordinating functional goals to the enterprise benefit. This requires clear-thinking leadership and confidence in the targeted outcomes. It is up to the program owner to ensure that the CEO is equipped to take this position.

Dealing with barriers — it's about people

The psychology of change should always be expected to crop up.

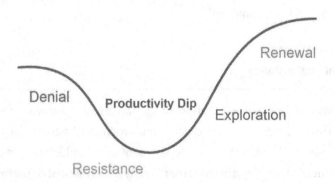

People need time to come to terms with change, and change does not really hit until a person becomes personally involved. The phases of Denial, Resistance, Exploration and Renewal, or Acceptance, will cover an amount of time that varies by individual and circumstance, but the phases will occur and it is important to recognise that they will arise despite careful planning because people will feel threatened by change.

The feeling of being threatened arises for three primary reasons.

People don't mind change, they mind being changed

People may perceive they are going to have to change for any number of reasons, such as:

- Existing investment
- Inertia
- Uncertain future
- Existing knowledge no longer valued, need for new learning
- Loss of power or influence

People are control oriented

Who is most comfortable with matters the way they are? People do not like the feeling of losing control over their lives, it causes stress, and stress goads people into action. When people get stressed they try and increase their level of control and if they are normally control-oriented they become tyrannical in their resistance.

People do not fear change, they fear loss

People will routinely say 'I don't mind change, change is good', they know this is expected of them. But when they realise that they will actually lose influence, power, position, or even their current job they will fear that loss, especially when they do not know how the organisation will treat them, whether they will be valued any longer, whether their contribution will continue to be respected.

To deal with the inevitable reactions it is important to work out who is threatened by the change and pre-empt their reaction as much as possible

Resistance may be short or long term, but it is important that it be dealt with directly as and when it is detected.

Inoculating barriers

To inoculate is to prevent something happening or diminish its effect by acting before the event. It is possible to inoculate against the psychological reactions to impending change. The following actions are good basic change management activities—some of which reflect points documented previously—but now the idea is to be proactive so that the barriers are never erected to a significant height.

- Involve
- Convey organisational need
- Identify WIIFMs
- Urgency
- Empathy
- Support mechanisms
- Extended change team
- Direct approach to resisters

Involve

Stakeholder involvement is an accepted principle so that commitment can be obtained and multiple perspectives can be dealt with; however, there is another reason for stakeholder involvement and that is to inoculate against the fear of change. Involvement makes people feel that they have some influence over what is occurring, that their opinions are being listened to, and it gives them greater knowledge of what will happen which can dispel the worst fears.

Convey organisational need

There must be a clearly articulated reason for the business change and the targeted benefits.

Most people can be quite altruistic if given the opportunity. If they really understand why the organisation needs to make a change then they will quite likely support it, even if it may be detrimental to their own interests. It is up to leadership to appeal to people's better instincts and articulate the business need.

Identify WIIFMs

'What's in it for me?' If altruism is not enough then find a reason for people to buy in because of some personal advantage they may receive. This advantage may not outweigh the disadvantages, but it gives them a rationale to buy in, to not lose face. If they believe that the change is inevitable they will probably accept the WIIFM as the reason to support the change.

Create urgency

As explained previously, momentum is essential and this is maintained by a sense of urgency. The sponsor creates a sense of urgency by explaining the business benefits that are sought and the threats to the business if change is not made and those benefits are not achieved.

A careful balance is required between a necessary sense of urgency and the need not to compromise the design of new processes by placing speed and deadlines ahead of getting the optimum process design—which requires sense-making and continual design review and improvement. For this reason it is best not to unduly emphasise the urgency at the program level, and only to build up a sense of urgency once business requirements for each process project have been reviewed by stakeholders.

Display empathy

Change is about people; people need their issues to be understood by those with power over them. Understanding their issues requires empathy. Good difficult changes often witness empathic leadership, because this enables people to come to terms with the change and support it. In modern times, dictating change and lacking empathy will often lead to resistance and rejection.

Provide support mechanisms

People need to know who they can turn to in order to seek guidance and support when a change is coming. Telephone numbers, email addresses and websites need to be well publicised, and people need confidence that communications will be confidential. If people will lose their jobs there must be clear strategy as to what help people will receive from the organisation and how they can access it.

Approach resisters directly

Sometimes there is validity in the barrier, it represents a valid objection that needs to be addressed, so keep an open mind. If it arises before roll out during the design phase there is still time to adjust the proposal. If the objection is personal then probing will encourage the objector to re-examine his/her assumptions and find a reason to differentiate from past experiences and find reasons to support the proposal. This happens because they feel they have been genuinely listened to and recognised as an individual. The majority of people are altruistic and will support a change for a greater good even though they may be disadvantaged, so long as their loss has been acknowledged and every attempt made to minimise it.

Extended change team

For roll out the team needs to be extended to include a transition team. The Transition Team will usually comprise front-line managers and the supervisors of all groups impacted by the change. The core team prepares roll out materials such as videos, slides, website references and handouts which it presents to the transition team—providing each team member with a set. At a specific time, all transition team members hold meetings with their groups of impacted people at which they go through the rollout materials and answer questions.

This avoids the problem of rumours arising if announcements are not synchronised.

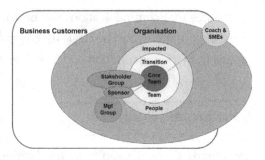

The diagram shows a complete program organisation structure that incorporates the transition team.

It also portrays the management and support groups and roles that are needed in program management.

Note that other people in the organisation and customers must also be considered in change management planning, they will be impacted indirectly by a drop in productivity as the impacted people become distracted by the roll out.

Leadership of change

As well as good management, change requires good leadership. The following diagram defines the signs of good change leadership:

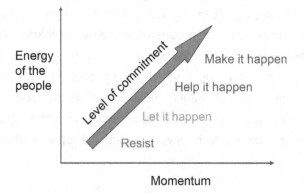

It is the role of change leaders to get people's commitment to the top level, in spite of all of the barriers.

The personalities of the people involved in process programs and those of the senior stakeholders are most important in terms of the effectiveness of change leadership. If there is conflict amongst these people, those opposed to the change will use it to advantage in discrediting the change. This means the CEO or most senior person in the organisation and the Program Owner must demonstrate outstanding leadership so that people know the change is going to happen, why it will happen, and what the benefits will be.

The program team led by the Program Manager needs to provide the senior leaders with the necessary support to ensure they can lead effectively, so that the change is effected with minimum disruption and for the maximum benefit. The team must provide scripts, emails and other materials for the leaders to use, they need to brief the leaders and ensure they understand all that is necessary for them to be confident in their position. Without such confidence there is a danger the leader may be challenged effectively and will turn on the program and decide it is a waste of time and expense.

Culture and processes

Organisations are predisposed to write processes that conform to existing culture. If an organisation is bureaucratic, its processes will be written to include many detailed forms, with checking activities, and approvals.

But processes may be used to change the culture. If the processes for the same organisation are written to require only enough information to enable the customer or user to complete the process, (and use the principles presented above) then the culture will change.

Implementing a process perspective will lead to a change in organisation structures and behaviours. Therefore, process programs can become the driver for culture change.

CHAPTER **12**

Process Organisation — Do We Need To Restructure?

Before considering implementation planning and roll out, there is a critical issue that needs to be discussed which is often left out of change planning and can become a major issue after the new process and system are implemented.

Implementing a new process and system not only affects the people who do the work but it may also affect who they report to and what the organisation structure should be to support the new process. If we are to make the best of all of the work that has been done, and for the process to operate as intended, an organisational restructure may be necessary.

Restructuring for processes

Up until the new process is implemented, the organisation structure has probably been based on functions, but now we wish to focus on how we deliver to the external customer using processes. Processes use functional technical skills and capabilities but they require a business structure for the processes to operate most effectively.

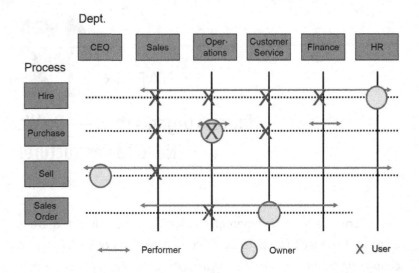

This is the dilemma that we face:

The performers do the work of the process and are presently situated within multiple functions. The users may be in one function or many. We need to choose a process owner who may or may not be a functional leader but who needs to be able to lead across functions without bias.

How do we restructure the organisation to manage the business using processes? Even if we introduce a process-led organisation, we will still need all of the technical skills and capabilities that are necessary to deliver our products, so we still need functional units for skilled activities.

Existing managers will probably say there is no issue, they will be responsible for their part of the process, as they are now. Whilst this is one way of introducing end-to-end processes into an organisation, and may prove quite effective initially, over time territorial considerations will come into play and functional concerns will begin to override enterprise process optimisation—functional managers will change their subprocesses for local improvement.

The preferred way of structuring a process organisation is to appoint business leaders as process managers and re-position functional managers as resource managers of skilled people completing activities that require a centre-of-excellence approach. As resource managers they are responsible for ensuring their people have the requisite skills and knowledge and will still manage their progression and remuneration.

However, the role of functional manager will appear to have been diminished in importance. Whilst difficult to convey, this does not remove the importance of functional managers—functional managers will still manage their people day-to-day. The role of the process manager is to manage the process and deal with systemic issues, they will not directly manage how the individual people in skilled functions do their work. For the benefit of the customers, the process managers will have authority over priorities as they can dictate the sequence of work to functional managers, but they will not manage how the people actually do the skilled work. However, process managers may manage new pools of low-skilled workers who can be put together as process support groups.

We already see this arrangement with support functions. As an example, business users specify to IT functions what systems they want and what the business requirements are, but the IT people do the detailed technical work. The same principle applies with process organisation. But we can also see the dangers, the IT functions in some organisations dictate what they will do and in what order—the technical strategies can even overtake the business strategies. It is important that the process managers have the authority to specify what is right for the customer, and can even demand better performance from functional teams.

What we need is both strong process management and high technical capabilities. We are not replacing one with the other.

There is another overlaid structure sometimes used in very large service organisations, that is, to set up individual account (customer) teams that include some (but not necessarily all) functional specialists and the account teams manage the sell, deliver and customer support processes for that account. The same principle can be applied with line of business organisational structures. There is still a need for process owners and managers to deal with process systemic matters across all accounts or lines of business but they are now supporting the account teams rather than the customers directly. There may still be functional teams for centre-of-excellence reasons but there will be fewer. The account or line of business managers will be the people ultimately responsible for price, delivery, quality, margins and customer satisfaction and therefore have over-riding authority.

This structure does not replace the basic organisational principles above, rather it adds a further dimension. If an organisation already has account management or line of business units they will likely welcome process reorganisation, but the potential for conflict between process and functional managers remains.

When to restructure

It is common in organisations for new leaders to reorganise first then change processes later. This is done so that the top leader has new managers to drive improvements and be responsible for improvements. This is how most new CEOs do it.

Moreover, when strategic improvements are needed, incumbent CEOs are likely to reselect senior leaders or shuffle them around.

However, changing the organisation structure as the first action may compound the functional silo problems, improvements may be limited to functional domains and as a result, processes are sub-optimised. Often this approach ends up with the CEO spending too much time mediating between functions.

To get lasting and the best possible improvement in organisational results, it is better to run an enterprise process program first. Afterwards new processes will cross functional boundaries and there are new ways of working, so what makes sense now?

With the new emphasis on delivering customer value, cross-functional teams may make more sense than traditional functional hierarchies.

As discussed above, functional managers are still essential to provide skills and training and professional governance, but their roles are now more 'resource managers', and process managers manage day-to-day activities.

However, operational managers are territorial, often Delivery has the lion's share of people and carries great influence as a result. For service organisations, Delivery may dictate what is offered to customers. So delivery operational managers have a lot to lose with a process reorganisation, and restructuring to give power to new process manager roles can be hard to implement. As a result, it can be disruptive and the strength of feeling can delay or even prevent reorganisation. The danger is that processes are innovated but the right organisation is never implemented, operational managers take ownership of subprocesses and overall process ownership is lost.

There are two restructure strategies:

Post-process implementation reorganisation

Leave operational managers with operational authorities and responsibilities, allocate process roles as additional roles and responsibilities to senior operational managers. Form an executive/ steering group (to include process owners) for monthly reporting by process managers (this is not the process program group, this is an operational group after process implementation), use this group to move power to process manager roles. And finally, reorganise after a settling in period.

With this strategy, conflicts will occur between process and operational managers, conflicts may rumble for some time and be covert and disruptive. If the culture is good enough, managers may resent disruption, and the better process role people will suggest reorganisation.

The CEO must be onside and approve this strategy, and the reasons for it, and then act when enough support emerges. The risk is that functional leaders could push the CEO to drop the strategy.

This strategy is often the default strategy because the implications of the process program are not well thought through and a systems view is not taken.

Reorganisation as part of implementation

The first task is to select process owners for each process. These roles will most likely be additional to people's existing roles. It would be unusual to recruit new senior managers into new process roles, although, this could be warranted if the organisation is large enough. If allocation is made internally it is important to select senior leaders who have the capability and willingness to work across functional boundaries, because a process owner has an enterprise role not a functional role.

The process owner selects a process manager, or takes on the role as well in a smaller organisation. Performers' work is reorganised to support the new process, performers' reporting lines are changed to the new process manager if needed, which impacts on the functional managers' teams. The new structure is implemented at go-live as the Process Manager assumes responsibility for the process.

The feeling that 'my team needs to be with me' has to be overcome if people are grouped into co-located process groups yet still have functional resource managers. If people stay in functional locations it may assist with maintaining skills and knowledge and the new system will be an enterprise system that is accessible from any location within the organisation. These are difficult issues that often take a great deal of time to resolve during implementation planning and a great deal will depend upon the resolve of the senior leadership.

Process roles do not have to be full-time, they may just be another 'hat' to wear. The simplest approach is to select individuals for the process roles based upon their capabilities and potential, regardless of their current roles.

A less disruptive approach may be to allocate process roles to functional leaders and managers as additional roles so long as they are educated in the process approach. This can be less than ideal as they may not be sufficiently business oriented to make good process owners or managers and may not be able to move away from their functional view. For this reason there should be a formal selection process so that their suitability can be assessed.

The advantage of this strategy is a shorter duration change period but a more disruptive one. It needs strong CEO leadership and a change of culture as a key driver. To succeed, it is essential to get senior leaders' acceptance and proactive support, and as new process owners they have a stake in success.

This strategy is more likely to realise all business benefits but make sure people are suited to the new roles.

Process Roles

Process owner

- Owns the process, supports it, nurtures it, and provides the organisational 'umbrella'
- Selects the Process Manager
- Provides process tools, including information systems
- Provides Process Manager training
- Measures process effectiveness
- Monitors customer value
- Supports process improvement
- Does not manage the project or the process

Selecting a Process Owner

Chose an executive or someone widely known and respected who has authority and influence. They must be able to take on a role that goes across functions, they need to be capable of and inclined towards becoming a process champion.

The BPM program owner needs to specify expectations and responsibilities of the role.

Process manager

- Manages the process and its platform
- Deals with systemic issues
- Reports on the process performance and key performance indicators (KPI)
- Provides user support and training
- Provides user help support. This may be in- or outsourced.
- Facilitates some connecting activities
- Schedules and runs process reviews
- Identifies process constraints and improvement potential
- Recommends capacity improvements if required
- Manages process improvement teams
- Ensures ISO and/or other quality certification

Selecting a Process Manager

The person chosen must have the strength to work across functions and operate by influence. The ideal characteristics for the person in this role are: people leader, customer oriented, consultative, technology savvy but not a 'techie', methodical, analytical, open-minded.

The process program will specify expectations and responsibilities.

User

Someone who uses the process to secure the required process output or outcome. The user initiates an 'instance' or 'case' which requires one complete cycle of the process.

Performer

A person (or team) who is responsible for completing a particular activity for every process instance. A process performer typically has a functional or technical skill or knowledge that suits them to perform that particular activity.

Customer

An external person who receives value from the process. A customer has a different perspective to those inside the organisation and is often best able to describe process inadequacies, but not necessarily inefficiencies. Be sure to determine their measurement of value and they should respond to process improvement.

CHAPTER **13**

Implementation — Tight Discipline Needed

No matter how good the process and system design and build are the project may fail if the implementation is poor. If the new process and system are rejected, or avoided, or only partially implemented the intended business benefits will not be achieved and the program will fall into disrepute.

The most likely reasons for failure will be inadequate change management. Also, if the process and system have significant errors or shortcomings revealed after go-live, users will complain bitterly, especially if there are no support mechanisms in place to rectify these issues.

Implementation planning and pilot

Implementation planning and pilot must be completed before roll out and go-live. The process for this phase is as follows.

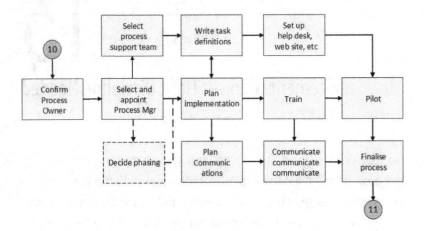

Confirm process owner/appoint process manager

The Process Owner and Process Manager may already have been identified, but if not, the decisions need to be made now. The Project Leader may take on the Process Owner role as they were selected because they are the person who will receive the primary business benefit of the new process and system. The Process Owner will then identify a key user of the process to become the Process Manager.

The alternative is to select people who have not been involved in the project—this is acceptable but it must be done at the beginning of implementation planning so they influence the implementation and come up to speed with the new process and system.

Decide phasing

For large processes and systems it may be decided to implement them incrementally by subprocess so as to spread the workload and facilitate user acceptance. Two or three separate implementations are planned and executed.

This approach may be reflected right back through the process and system design and development, with each part of the process being a different project. This is particularly useful if the first part of the process solution is uncertain and needs to be clear before the rest of the process can be worked on.

Plan implementation

Implementation planning covers the entire period from solution completion through to go-live, including support set up, pilot and rollout. A more detailed rollout plan will be prepared prior to go-live, implementation planning is at a strategic level and maps out the integration of IT, change management, communications and training activities. These have to be synchronised and cohesive, have momentum and clarity of actions and goals.

Planning is best handled by someone with project scheduling experience, who integrates information from the project team and process manager and support people.

Process support

The pilot will be supported by the project team. Support for the process after go-live will be provided by the Process Manager and support for the system by existing IT Support.

The Process Manager may select key users in different parts of the organisation who respond to user queries, leaving the Process Manager to deal with systemic issues.

IT Support will respond to system problems and may in turn refer back to the analyst who was involved in the project—who will now be working on a different project.

If the user population is large and the process and system are complex a dedicated support team may needed. More likely, there will be a support team for all processes and BPM systems as the program progresses because of how important the process infrastructure has become and there may be common modules operating across different processes and systems.

Once the support strategy and the people have been chosen, complete role definitions. Support email addresses, phone numbers and website content need to be provided and be ready for go-live. Any training for support people will be provided by the project team.

Communications

During implementation planning, communications channels will be selected and a timeline prepared. Detailed planning and communications writing will occur during the rollout period.

Use a professional communications person if one can be assigned for the implementation, who will know multiple communications channels to use and will have good writing skills, and will be able to integrate implementation information into other organisational publications such as newsletters and websites.

Pilot

We have already discussed the need for testing, just as important is the need for a pilot. When a system goes live, users expect it to be perfect and even a small number of bugs or process errors will cause an adverse reaction; however, when users know they are part of a pilot they know the purpose of the pilot is to find and correct bugs and errors and will feel they are doing a good job if they discover and report them.

A pilot should be conducted by a user group that represents the entire user population. For example, if the user population is employed in 10 or 12 business units, 2 or 3 can be selected for the pilot. There needs to be more than one so that different ways of using the process and system are tested.

A good pilot identifies all shortcomings which can be fixed before the operational process and system go live, and consequently, user acceptance levels after go-live will be high.

All of the necessary actions for rollout and go-live are completed at a smaller scale for the pilot. The system should be isolated from other systems at this stage as it may be necessary to revert to previous methods if major changes are needed. This means some simpler, even manual, methods may be used for providing data as integration has not yet occurred. Information may be downloaded from other enterprise systems and held in a local database for access by the pilot system. Aside from integration aspects, the system should be as close to a final operational system as possible.

As feedback is received during the pilot a change log should be maintained, documenting every comment received with action decisions, action assignments and completion dates. The types of feedback are:

Action: fix bug, small improvement changes, and format changes.

Query: reported issue cannot be reproduced, investigate further.

Defer: too big a change for this version, held over for consideration for inclusion in next version.

Reject: not considered valid or not appropriate for most users, or not worthwhile as value is too small compared with the cost of change.

Run the pilot for the planned period even if feedback slows right down.

Finalise process

During the pilot changes are actioned according to the change log. Major changes should be avoided, only minor changes should be dealt with otherwise the pilot must be repeated.

By the end of the pilot, or shortly thereafter, all changes must be completed, system tests repeated and the system and support materials updated to the final process and system that will go live.

Rollout

During rollout new process and system websites are published online; intended users are informed about the new process and system, given handout materials and given website addresses for further information, feedback and system access. The rollout must be completed as quickly as possible so that the period of instability between contemplating giving up the old methods and accepting the new is as short as possible. This is the period during which productivity will fall.

This is the rollout subprocess:

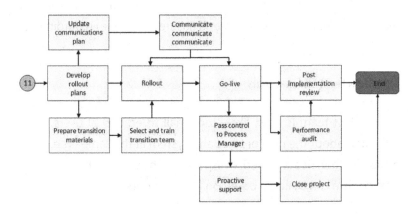

Rollout planning

Publication of the go-live date should be kept as late as possible so that there is a very high probability of meeting the deadline. Up until then, references to the go-live date should be broad, for example, 'in the last quarter' or 'early in the new year'. The date should be announced once the detailed rollout plan is completed.

The rollout should occur in no longer than one month. Process rollout includes training/education, demonstrations or announcements, user group meetings, any organisational changes, individual interviews, putting up or updating support websites, stakeholder notifications, publication of policy changes, announcement of Process Owner and Manager and support arrangements.

System rollout includes preparing databases, writing any scripts, data migration, final system testing, load testing, any integration completions and cutover to the new system on go-live.

The preferred layout for the plan is by day. Actions that take longer than a day will be shown multiple times. This enables the project leader to monitor progress easily and ensures everyone is coordinated.

Transition team and materials

The project team is most likely too small to enable all users to be informed about the new process and system at the same time. If the announcement is staggered, whispers run ahead of the briefings and antagonism can build up based on false rumours.

To solve this problem, the project team prepares presentations and handouts and brief front-line supervisors all in one session. The supervisors are given a date and time shortly before go-live to meet with their teams and pass on the information about the new process and system. This way all users learn about the change at the same time.

Rollout

On go-live date IT makes the system available to users online, the process becomes mandatory and previous process methods are withdrawn.

Control is taken over by the Process Manager and the project team provides support to the Process Manager for a limited period, typically a week or two. All user queries are directed to the Process Manager for the first few weeks until use of the new process settles down, then users are redirected to key users and help desks for ongoing first level support.

Communications

Throughout the rollout period regular communications should ensure that everyone is aware of what change is occurring, why, who is impacted and how, as well as how to get more information and provide feedback.

Communications convey the business reason for change and why it is urgent to make the change. It provides a sense of identity to the new process and system and attempts to build a sense of anticipation and excitement and reduces the feeling of threat.

Communications also go out to the wider company audience so that people know what is happening. At the same time, customers are warned to expect a brief productivity dip followed by an improved service.

Close project

Once the Process Manager is coping with operation of the new process the project can be, and should be, closed down. Any further changes will either be handled by the Process Manager, working with the support team including IT, or they will be listed for inclusion in the next version.

It is important to close down the project promptly so that resources may be redeployed and not frittered away doing small updates to the process and system.

Post-implementation review

Two to six months after implementation, a post-implementation review meeting is convened by the Process Owner and all people who were involved in the project and the key people who have been involved in the process and system after go-live are invited.

The purpose of the meeting is to recognise and document the learning that has occurred which may help future projects to be more efficient and effective.

The Process Manager collects and publishes all of this information.

Performance audit

To assist the post-implementation review, and to see how results contributed to the business benefits targeted by the original business strategy that initiated the process program, a formal audit may be conducted by an internal auditor. This should be completed shortly before the meeting date and forwarded to the Process Owner for review and tabling at the meeting.

This completes the coverage of process programs and projects. We will now take a brief look at process costing and ongoing process improvement and then look at overall strategic considerations for the future.

CHAPTER 14

Costing, — How Process Analysis Enables Better Cost Management

Resource usage times and rates can be attached to activities and extended to arrive at activity costs. Labour and direct materials can easily be allocated whether using conventional cost accounting methods or activity-based methods. But with activity-based costing, other costs for each activity, such as consumables, power, and so on, can also be assigned using cost drivers, that is, a measurement that relates consumption to activity, such as machining time for the allocation of power and tooling costs. More overhead costs tend to be directly assigned to activities than is the case with conventional cost accounting. Total activity costs can then be accumulated by product/ service and deducted from sales price to arrive at gross margin or contribution. This is the margin that would be lost if the service were no longer delivered, other costs remain as fixed overheads to support other services.

Conventional cost allocation methods share some of these principles, such as determining direct labour costs (typically from task times), but overhead costs are assigned to cost centres first for all expense types and are then allocated using a general measure—typically labour or machine time—to arrive at a total cost to compare with price and derive a net margin. Because costs are pooled by cost centre, individual cost drivers are not used and product/service costs are distinctly less accurate and are always open to contention.

Conventional cost accounting uses 'standard' product/service costs and measures variances from these standard costs. This approach can led to wrong decisions, for example, improving production times lowers overhead recovery (assuming overheads are recovered on production times, which is the normal approach) resulting in adverse cost variances, which appears to indicate something has gone wrong. In fact, labour and variable overhead costs will have reduced, and fixed overheads are unchanged. If the costing system differentiates between variable and fixed overheads there will still be under-recovery of fixed costs.

Process costing offers better insight into product/service costs and margins and how variations in activities drives costs. There is a more intuitive understanding of costs amongst production people and, as a result, a better awareness of costs and the effects of process improvement and where to focus on cost reduction. More importantly, process costing is a sounder basis on which to make business decisions about product/service range, prices, order acceptance priorities, promotion and investment.

There are at least four methods used for process costing. They all exist to overcome the deficiencies of conventional cost accounting methods, and support particular ways of looking at processes. These methods are better suited to business management, as distinct from financial management, and so these methods are often operated within business units rather than within the finance department.

Business unit managers may ask for support from Finance to undertake any analysis, but the business unit owns the method and system.

Activity-Based Costing (ABC)

ABC is a permanent ongoing system collecting costs and activity-driver information. The system produces reports with activity and process costs and margins for products or services.

ABC automatically collects costs over time and therefore cost and profit trends can be constantly monitored and related back to cost/profit improvement initiatives.

Activity-Based Management (ABM)

ABM is a snapshot approach that estimates resource allocation by interviewing operational people and asking them to allocate their time across activities, merely by assessment rather than direct measurement. The process cost accumulations are completed based on these time assessments. This approach suits service organisations where the majority of service costs relates to people time.

Once people costs and contributions to overhead and profit have been established, hypotheses are developed as to how to reduce costs and increase profits—which can then be implemented and a new snapshot exercise undertaken to establish whether an improvement has been realised.

ABM is quicker and cheaper to establish than ABC.

Lean Accounting

Lean accounting focuses on value stream profitability. It assumes reducing costs enables improvements in capacity, enabling greater throughput and greater revenues and therefore more profit. Individual activity and product costs are not calculated; rather, the emphasis is on value streams and directs actions at enabling growth and improving customer value.

'Box scores' are widely used in reporting. Key indicators are shown for operational performance, capacity utilisation and financial results, the latter focused on value stream profitability.

Lean Accounting is used to identify excessive cost and where to focus improvement efforts. Lean accounting systems are much simpler than cost accounting and ABC systems as they are more strategic in their focus and do not require the same level of detail and analysis.

Lean accounting is usually associated with lean (six sigma) programs because conventional cost accounting results are frequently contradictory to the aims and achievements of lean programs.

Throughput Cost Accounting (TCA), based on the Theory of Constraints (TOC)

TOC is focused on reducing the bottleneck, or constraint, to enable increased throughput. TCA assumes all costs (except direct materials) to be fixed, including labour—and inventory asset valuations only includes material costs. TCA looks at sales less variable (material) costs to yield contribution, less fixed (all operational) costs to yield profit. TCA also looks at return on assets. The incentive for local optimisation, which traditional cost accounting creates, is removed, as the only way to increase return on assets is to increase sales, reduce operational costs or reduce assets, particularly inventories.

Another advantage of TCA is that it better reflects cash flow generation, which is often the critical survival factor and growth prerequisite in many businesses.

As with Lean Accounting, TCA is simple in concept and application, but supports a TOC business management approach which better reflects how a business really makes profits.

Which of the above costing methods an organisation should select depends on the strategies and programs adopted by the business. ABM, Lean Accounting and TCA are all relatively straightforward to implement and can replace expensive cost accounting systems. ABC is more complicated, but as with the other methods, yields information that is much more aligned with the needs of business management. There may even be merit in using more than one of the methods to get a wider perspective on decision making.

CHAPTER **15**

Process Improvement — Continual Refinement

Process Improvement is a generic phrase which is sometimes intended to include BPM. In the current context it is referring to refinement activities that occur frequently and without end, as opposed to the transformational programs of limited duration that are the focus of BPM.

Processes can always be improved. After a process program has introduced new innovated processes, people think about what else could be done, it is almost instinctive to suggest further changes because beneficial change has been proved to be possible. However, if this reaction is not capitalised on fairly quickly, other operational matters will crowd out time and the opportunity will fade.

Aside from team suggestions there are many drivers for process improvement. Customer feedback or new requirements may necessitate process changes; the competitive environment can force a search for improvements, although, it is better to be the change leader—indeed the introduction of new products or services may be the driver.

The process manager is responsible for ensuring that process improvement is achieved, and to do that, a process is required. The process can be implemented as part of a broader improvement program or it may just be a regular operational matter.

The process manager must listen for suggestions from process users, process performers, customers and other stakeholders. There should be a well-advertised means of providing feedback, a phone number, email address or website.

The process will be centred on a regular meeting of the process team for review and discussion of improvements. Drivers and suggestions will be tabled for discussion and ideas for improvement generated. The ideas will be evaluated and tested between meetings and decisions and actions agreed at the next meeting.

Sometimes rewards may be offered and given for good suggestions but it is better if the culture is conducive to making suggestions.

If there is a formal process improvement program there may be a coach who will work with teams initially, until a satisfactory performance level is established. There are several formal process improvement methodologies that are used by organisations.

- Six Sigma programs use statistical techniques to provide focus for improvement efforts by eliminating waste. Training for team members is necessary and important in establishing the culture.
- Lean programs have built on Six Sigma with more innovative expectations and the aim of eliminating all non-value activities.
- A customer value focus is the core aim of Customer Experience Management (CEM), with a focus on doing the right things for the customer rather than just doing things right.

There is a trend towards blurring the line between BPM and process improvement. The latter has become more project focused and innovation added as a goal. The organisation needs to be clear about its objectives and the strategy to reach them, and select the methodology that is most appropriate.

CHAPTER 16

The Goal, the Benefit and the Risks

You have implemented multiple, radically redesigned processes and supporting workflow systems; your people are now adept at BPM and continue with process projects; process managers are managing their processes and further improving their processes and systems with their process teams. You may have upgraded your original BPMS and have provided workflow access to previously existing enterprise systems, your major databases are continuously updated by process flows and your enterprise information is integrated.

How does your organisation look now? In what way is it better than before? Is it providing better returns? Was it worth all the time and cost?

The goal

Organisational characteristics

Your organisation could be like this:

-   The processes are the day-to-day business – what work is done and how it is done is unambiguous and consistent and everything that is done adds value.

- Processes are results-focused – all work contributes to the outputs of the organisation, either directly as customer value or indirectly to manage the business efficiently.
- Processes are differentiation – reputation comes from quality of delivery and the organisation is recognised for its excellence.
- Customer value comes from the processes – processes are adaptable so only activities that add value for the specific customer are undertaken and all activities add value.
- Processes are measured – BPMS delivers comprehensive process reporting, process managers receive measurements that enable them to identify constraints and improvements.
- Processes encourage collaboration – people see themselves as part of a team and value chain, rather than as functionaries only responsible for their job.
- A systems viewpoint and approach has been adopted – there is awareness of how everything connects and that actions have impacts elsewhere, so there is much better problem prevention.
- Staff are focused, effective, and efficient – work is productive with minimal supervision.
- Teams are self-organising – with reduced supervision communications are horizontal and teams sort out internal imbalances.
- People are proactive – with good communications teams are responsible and proactive and individuals feel released to do better.
- The organisation is nimble and able to survive external change – proactive teams respond to changing requirements and circumstances.

- Customer-orientation is natural – focus is on the customer, turf conflict is minor and those who do not contribute are eased out.
- Teams are self-improving – teams look for and implement improvement all the time, they do not wait to be told.
- Situation leadership arises – flatter organisation and effective delegation leads to knowledge-based, self-identifying, situational leadership.
- Satisfaction and commitment are the norm – teams are proud of the value delivered to customers and committed to the organisation and their teams.

The benefit

The benefit to the organisation is considerable: improved throughput capacity with the same resources, improved reputation leading to increased throughput and revenues, greater margins, and better profit. The whole organisation 'hums' as it works collaboratively with less inter-factional politics and non-productive distractions. People feel better about working in the organisation, have a sense of pride in customer service; they feel valued themselves and more involved in what goes on and so are committed to their roles, teams and the organisation.

There will always be problems, people issues in particular, but the organisation is more resilient and better able to deal with issues.

Culture

The culture of the organisation is different, the comparison with a traditional organisation is stark:

Traditional	*Process*
- Job focused	- Role focused
- Functional allegiance	- Process team allegiance
- Internal power rivalry	- External focus
- Individual rewards	- Team rewards
- Professional skills	- Professional skills
- Personal achievement	- Contribution
- Status leadership	- Situational leadership

Note that the same or better level of professional skills is required and this is why functional leadership is still required for resource management. Process and functional management has to cooperate to produce the right results, effective leadership must ensure this happens.

This all sounds great, but are there problems? Indeed there are—we need to consider the risks.

The risks

Implications of anti-fragility[xxv]

The world is complex and changing at an ever increasing rate, we are in a time of revolution. It is not possible for organisations to plan for the future in the way they used to because there are too many unexpected and disruptive events. A planned future may work for a while, but eventually someone has a better idea and the organisation is out-flanked.

The question becomes, how can organisations be sufficiently flexible and perceptive to identify changes and react quickly enough to stay in the race?

One viewpoint, and sometimes the reality, is that processes embed the status quo in an organisation which ceases to be sufficiently flexible to survive in the medium and long term. Effective processes may lead to an entrenched sense of certainty and superiority which ultimately betrays the organisation. This is a major risk for which leadership must have a coping strategy. The goal is not to achieve a new static business model, but to achieve a model that operates efficiently but can also recognise emerging patterns in a chaotic environment and act to capitalise on them.

Aside from futurists and market researchers, the people most likely to identify emerging trends are those closest to the customers and with an interest in the particular technologies used by the industry. When emerging patterns are identified, the organisation needs to be able to react quickly, breaking existing methods and abandoning investments to pursue new technologies and products or services. This is difficult, it is uncomfortable for an organisation that is presently profitable, with a sense of achievement and position in the industry, to accept uncertain and uncomfortable new directions.

Quite clearly, the strategic awareness, objectives and assumptions of the organisation will need to be up to the task. Strategies will have to be constantly re-examined for currency, and leadership will have to be prepared to accept greater risk in new, destabilising investments in order to survive and prosper.

What does this all mean for processes? There are concepts behind process management we have discussed which help reduce the complacency which creates fragility:

1. The concept of systems thinking awakens people to the idea of looking all around rather than focusing on their little operational box. It stimulates interest in the wider world and facilitates earlier recognition of relevant external change.

2. The concept of throughput as the profit generator reduces excessive analysis focused on individual products and services, the organisation has to achieve an overall throughput rate and is more open to new ways of generating throughput.

3. The theory of constraints with an assumption of spare capacity provides change resource and the never-ending search for the new constraint will enhance awareness of changing influences.

4. Focus on customer value will help identify changes in customer requirements (but will not help identify disruptive technologies which just take away customers).

5. Process measurement enables quicker identification of adverse process trends and delegation to process teams enables quicker reactions (but ditto).

6. The design principle of alternative process routes for different customer requirements will help identify changing requirements (but ditto).

The latter three points underline the fact that a process infrastructure will not protect against disruptive or 'black swan'[xxvi] changes. Nassim NicholasTaleb [(Ibid.)] suggests the need is for organisational robustness. The concepts of scenario planning and chaos theory point to a similar need. This leads to strategies of flexible rather than rigid investment, of delegation to front-line people so as to engage the maximum number of minds and watchers in the problem and a culture of robust debate and avoidance of sacred cows.

So, it is all about how processes are implemented, how they are viewed and what the culture in the organisation promotes.

Processes do not have to reduce robustness, but they can if the leadership is unaware of the risks of fragility and does not act to embrace anti-fragility thinking. Process design will not predict a black swan event or discontinuity, and a watchful eye on emerging alternative customer solutions is needed. It appears, at this time, process management is really only able to support existing business models and is unlikely to predict new models, although changing patterns in process usage may alert management to a discontinuity.

The secret lies in encouraging stakeholders to keep an ear to the ground because they feel involved and they are interested, and then for leaders to be open to warnings even if they make them feel uncomfortable or dismissive. Good implementation of process culture will have this result.

Functional process work

It is common for a functional leader to be the first to focus on processes and to start a program to improve their processes. But some of these processes are in fact subprocesses covering the activities in their function within a cross-functional process.

If this is the case, it is up to the BPM consultant, the project leader or a functional leader/subprocess owner with an understanding of the benefit of an enterprise view to ensure that the other subprocesses within the enterprise process are identified at a high level, and that stakeholders in tangential subprocesses are involved in the (sub) process project, so that information interfaces and activities between functional subprocesses can be properly connected. If this is done there is a good chance that the involvement of the stakeholders for the rest of the process will result in the subsequent commission of a project or projects to improve some of the other sub processes. Once this occurs, senior management should spot the osmosis trend (or the BPM consultant or leader calls their attention to it) and call for the whole process to be reviewed, building on work to date. This may result in rework as an enterprise view is not the same as the aggregation of functional views, but this is a way of leading the organisation to a pan-enterprise understanding of processes over time.

If an enterprise approach is never reached, then processes will always be sub-optimised at the functional subprocess level and many of the benefits of an enterprise process program will never be achieved— and the opportunity for radical redesign will be lost. Individual functional leaders will be content with the results but the organisation misses an opportunity.

Inadequate structural adjustment

Even if an enterprise program is the vehicle for process change it is still possible that work is merely assigned to existing job positions and no structural reform takes place. There will be benefits, and the use of an enterprise IT system will help reduce inter-functional barriers and promote collaboration. However, functional allegiances will prevail and there is less chance of inculcating a common focus on customer value.

The other risk is that activity performers will become or remain isolated, merely seeing their activities on their screen and not communicating with other performers as they do not have a process view.

This can only be fixed or avoided by senior leadership taking a firm grip on the process strategy, discovering the potential for business gains from restructuring after process redesign, and declaring a determination to secure the maximum benefit of process redesign through restructure, then following through.

Inadequate sponsorship

Any change program that has inadequate sponsorship is in danger of underachievement or failure, regardless of how good project leaders are. If the organisation sees a program or project as functionally driven, then territorial politics come into play. If the functional leader is capable of accepting that the enterprise view is the way to the best solution, they may have enough influence and standing to ensure that the solution to functional process work as described above is achieved. However, if the sponsorship is directed at functional political advantage, then the project is vulnerable to adverse political influence on the organisation's senior leader (CEO or similar) and other leaders who will not benefit from the project, and reasons will be surfaced and promoted to cancel or diminish the project.

Industry IT solutions

Unique industry IT application solutions proliferate, they existed before BPMS and have evolved to include workflow management as BPM came to the fore. Sometimes it is easier for an organisation to adopt an industry IT solution and for their processes to be adapted to the often complicated software preferred ways of working.

The risks of allowing IT to lead process projects has been dealt with previously; unfortunately, many large organisations do abdicate their business management change responsibilities to the IT vendor. If this is not the case, and business leaders are firmly in charge of the process program then this approach can be legitimate, but it is still important to go through process design so that the organisation understands the gap between their preferred processes and those enforced by the software.

The biggest risk is that the software has inadequate workflow management, merely being a traditional database program, and the huge gains to be had from a BPM approach are not realisable. Database system analysis typically includes function workflows, so IT may point to these charts and claim they are process flows, but they are not end-to-end and they are not part of a workflow management system. They are designed as individual activities that the user has to call up, there is no proactive movement of tasks by the system, and they are not process designs.

Existing enterprise IT solutions

Investment in existing enterprise IT applications may dictate that process work use the functionality of these systems.

This can work, process management can overlay existing enterprise applications and ensure the value of the investment is not lost; indeed, it is extended.

Processes may even be designed to utilise existing enterprise systems' functionality, reducing or obviating the need for new systems.

The use of separate TO BE and SYSTEM designs is a good way of understanding the connection between process design and the use of the existing systems.

CHAPTER 17

The Future of Processes — Evolution or Revolution?

Penetration of BPMS

BPMS are constantly evolving as the vendors compete with each other to win business and as business discovers the potential for better business solutions based on technology improvements.

Overall, the scope for computerisation is reaching further and further into manual work arenas. The economics of BPMS is allowing processes with lower frequency of use to become economic—to computerise and automate—and people see the potential for making their working life easier and to improve their service delivery.

Very large organisations, such as tax and social welfare government agencies, have been steadily improving their service to citizens by evolving their online systems. The assumption today is that citizens are sufficiently computer literate to use computers, but they still maintain front offices that can help those who cannot cope and to provide access to computers for those who do not have internet access. However, internet access from smart phones is ensuring a generational change to ubiquitous use of online systems by citizens. Inevitably, there will be eventual consolidation of government-to-citizen front offices, further ensuring the increasing usability of citizen online systems.

Large retail organisations are going through a retailing revolution as online purchasing acquires a progressively larger share of consumer spending, ensuring that retailers are developing new online retailing systems. Restaurants are increasingly taking customer orders on tablet systems which are integrated with kitchen processes. Low-cost online ecommerce solutions allow small retailers to computerise their operations very easily. Everywhere you look, organisations are extending use of online systems.

Firstly this was just about customer interfaces, once a customer completed their actions the results needed to be passed to existing internal systems. But the change in the customer interface has driven an expectation of similar efficiency in back office systems and better customer service. This has driven BPM as larger organisations respond to customer demands for better service.

This is leading to a rapid infill of non-computerised manual activities so that organisations have fully integrated operational systems for end-to-end processes ending in customer value. New start-ups are computerising their processes from the beginning, there is enough low cost workflow management software available to do this.

This vision of totally integrated computerised processes is the key driving force behind the rise in the importance of BPM programs and the identification by business leaders of the importance of workflow management and delivery of customer value. At the same time, the computerisation of workflow is facilitating a response to customer demands for individualisation.

Case management

The individuality of customer requirements on service organisations leads progressively towards the use of case management. Case management is about identifying unique circumstances for individual customers and catering for their needs. This requires a flexibility of process and the ability to collect individual customer information.

To deal with case management the traditional BPMS functionality has been improved to include case management—the label iBPMS (intelligent BPMS) is being used to differentiate this and some other feature developments from previous BPMS. Two of the key new features of iBPMS are enabling completion of activities in a random order and ad hoc additional activities. These facilitate greater flexibility for the processing of individual cases.

However, the principles and methods of process design should be perfectly capable of specifying the need for, and solution to, case management needs. So the distinction of iBPMS from BPMS merely marks the evolutionary changes in process tools arising naturally as organisations evolve the reach of their process programs.

'Big data'

'Big data', or the useful analysis of large amounts of data to reveal actionable trends, is an emerging field of computing designed to respond to the need for business robustness in the face of unpredictable and disruptive changes. Because organisations are becoming so computerised they are collecting large amounts of data. Whilst this started as an administrative requirement to hold audit trails and proof of action, the information is a rich source for data mining to format information for future use.

BPMS are a source for much of the new data being collected by organisations. As operations are infilled with computer systems, all information is captured and available for analysis. However, for anti-fragility purposes, access is also needed to external data in domains from whence the unpredictable changes will come.

iBPMS provides linkages to, or incorporates analysis of, targeted data inputs. For now, these are principally of internal data. It remains to be seen whether 'big data' can respond to the need for external disruptive pattern detection, but it certainly offers great business potential for those who can provide solutions. Watch this space!

Mobile devices

Mobile devices are increasingly the preferred technology for systems access. This is a technical not a process issue. The same process design should work for fixed or mobile points of system access. However, the use of mobiles is part of the driving force towards ubiquitous computerised processes.

Value chain process integration

If you want to supply a major retailing chain there is a very good chance you will have to use their procurement systems. There is no reason not to integrate processes across organisations other than confidentiality and a sense of identity, and perhaps the need for flexibility in relationships in the face of competitive uncertainty. All the principles we have discussed about enterprise processes can be applied across organisations to integrate with suppliers, sub-contractors, outsourcers, channels to market and customers.

The Future

The future state picture is of enterprise and value chain processes implemented in workflow management systems, integrated with specialist enterprise operational systems and databases, with a drive towards collection and analysis of external information. This is happening by evolution.

However balance is needed between consistency of process and outputs, adaptability to the customer's individual needs, and unpredictable change, even discontinuities.

With the increase in rate of change and unpredictable discontinuities revolution may be necessary. The ability to handle the complexity of frequent change may pressure process thinking to accommodate unpredictability as a norm, which does not sit well with pre-specified processes. Case management sits along this line of development, but there is a lot further to go.

A key risk to organisations is that procedural instructions are essentially bureaucratic. Bureaucracy represents control[xxvii], control creates inflexibility. So any IT system and procedure, implemented at the task level, has the potential to create inflexibility and therefore vulnerability to discontinuities.

This re-enforces the view that processes should be defined at activity level. It also means that there is value in BPMS implementations working directly from the activity models, if the BPMS is smart enough to develop acceptable task detail automatically. This is a fundamental change to the methods espoused earlier in this book. The issue then is how to create confidence that local decision-making will reflect governance requirements if no procedures are directly specified by the business. The solution is not yet clear but must be a goal.

There are advantages in process designs and BPMS that allow local manipulation of activities, to create process flexibility. This will allow less specific, that is less restrictive, business requirements. This in turn will speed up process implementations and revisions, enabling quicker response to discontinuities.

But none of this will mean anything unless the right leadership, structures and culture are in place. This is the real revolution that is needed—in fact has started but still has a long way to go.

Whatever the direction it is clear that the ability for stakeholders to identify disruptive changes is key, and they will do this if they are sufficiently interested, committed to the organisation and feel that they will be heard and heeded. The moving of decision-making to the front-line that comes with implementing a real process culture is fundamental to creating the culture that will support dealing with dynamic change in the environment.

CHAPTER **18**

Next — What Are You Going To Do Now?

If you are a strategy and/or a program owner then you need to work on the program justification and getting it under way. Hopefully this book will help do this and the way is clear.

If you are a middle manager with a vision of what good processes can bring to your organisation there is work to do before you can start a process program. The first thing to recognise is you cannot do it on your own, so do not beat yourself up if you have failed to get a program moving so far.

Getting support

You need a sponsor, probably not just your boss, or the program would be under way already. You need someone with the power and influence at a senior level to get a program approved and to hold off disbelievers. This is very much about individual personality not necessarily roles, you need the right person to cultivate.

Senior people are always interested in something that will make their life easier, as are we all. So you have to understand how a process program could help them achieve their objectives and talk to them in a way that enables them to see how you can help them. Then they will be interested and you may be surprised at how quickly they can dispense with hierarchical attitudes and focus on how you can help them.

If you feel you do not have enough access to the right person then maybe you should try and bring together a 'community of interest' amongst your peers, convince them, and present your case collectively to the targeted sponsor.

Defining the business case

There must be a business case. To start with it a may just be a brief white paper that defines how a process program links to the organisational goals, objectives and strategies and what benefits might be achieved. Strategic alignment is essential for the program to get off the ground.

If this generates interest, a business case will follow which provides more detail—but do not get too specific as programs deal with uncertainty, you do not know what you are going to find. Talk in ranges rather than absolute numbers.

Do whatever the sponsor feels she/he needs to get CEO approval.

Managing up

As the situation evolves, it is up to you to keep driving it onwards, this means providing the sponsor with communication materials and insights. You are working on behalf of the organisation—effectively as an adjunct of the CEO's office, not in a functional role, because you

driving an enterprise approach. Assume that level of influence, if you do not have the necessary authority get the sponsor to do what is necessary, make it happen.

Good luck! Let me know how you get on, email me through my consulting website

http://businessprocessesaustralia.com.au

I am always interested to hear about peoples' experiences, there is always something new to learn.

Portfolio Management

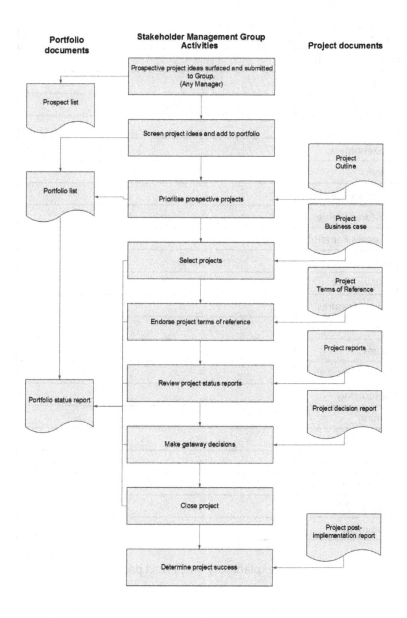

Project Outline

Item	Description	
Project Description		
Scope		
Sponsor	Title	Name
Customer		
Stakeholders		
Users		
Goals + Objectives		
Customer Value		
Business Benefits		
Risks		
Deliverables		
Value Measures		
CSFs		
Issues		
Constraints		
Resourcing		
Timing		
Responsibilities		
Revenue gains		
Incremental costs		
Technical Platform		
Comments		

See explanatory notes next page

Explanatory Notes

Distinguish between the project and the process. Comments are sought on both.

Project and version	The name of the project. It may be the name of a process or other project result. Version refers to version of this Outline.
Project Description	Up to 80 words, to outline what the project is about.
Scope	Define inclusions and exclusions for the project and the system that will implement the process, so that the scope is clear
Sponsor	The senior person who is recommending this project and may be providing budget cover.
Customer	The group of people which is the beneficiary of the result of this project once it is completed and the process or other result put into operation.
Stakeholders	Any persons or groups with an interest in, or who are impacted by, the results of the project or the project itself.
Users	Any persons or groups who will use the process delivered by the project, or other asset generated by the project.
Goals + Objectives	What the project and project results are intended to achieve.
Customer Value	The value the customer derives from the process or other project result.
Business Benefits	The benefits the organisation receives by investing in this project.
Value Measures	Measures that relate to the customer value and business benefits stated above, which will be used to judge the success of the project and of the process or other project result.
Risks	Any risks of the project and the process or other result to the organisation and stakeholders. These may be financial, operational, organisational, market, reputation, or any other dimension.
Deliverables	Specific, measurable, project deliverables.
CSFs	(Critical Success Factors). Things that have to happen in order for the project to succeed.
Issues	The issues that are driving this project.
Constraints	Policy, resourcing, financial, organisational, legal, social, environmental, or other factors that constrain how the project is to be delivered.

Resourcing	The primary resources that will be required for the project.
Timing	Preferred start date, duration and target completion date and any implications of delayed start or slippage. Also, any dependencies and their timing.
Major costs of project	People project time in person days, ball-park costs of asset purchases, other service costs and other purchases.
Revenue Gains	As a result of implementing the process or other project result, any increase in revenues for the organisation or unit within it.
Incremental Costs	As a result of implementing the process or other project result, any increase in costs for the organisation or unit within it.
Technical Platform	Any known technology platforms required for the process or other project result, including databases.
Comments	Any further comments that may assist the SMG in its understanding and assessment of the project.

Project Terms of Reference

Project Name	
Project Brief Name	
Project Description	
Organisational benefits	
Project Objectives	
Project Scope	
Does Include	
Does Not Include	
Project Deliverables	
Project Inputs	
Project Completion	
Measures of Success	
Marginal Costs	

Project Planning

Milestone Targets	

Project Organisation

Project Owner		
Project Manager		
Project Team		

Process Profile

Process:

Version:

Item	Description	
Customer		
Customer Need + Value		
Business Beneficiary		
Business Benefit		
Description		
Objective		
CSFs		
Performance Measures		
Trigger:		
Deliverable		
Completion		
Issues		
Constraints		
Throughput Metrics		
Technical Platform(s)		
Location		
Owner		
Performers		
Users		

Process Definition

Examples from project management

Required Information

1. Process Flowchart

2. Process Matrix

3. Description: (Describe the process)

> This process specifies the activities which occur prior to project planning. It seeks to ensure that there is a common understanding about the objectives of the project, documented in the charter, in order to facilitate the planning process. It sets expectations about the planning process timing and outcomes.

4. Objectives: (What the process aims to achieve)

> Formally launches the project and ensures a common understanding about the project in order to facilitate planning.

5. Process Inputs:

List any physical items and information that are input to the process and their source

> Any prior documents, including:
> - Business proposal
> - Business case
> - Initial scope statement or project concept or brief
> - Feasibility study

6. Process Outputs/Deliverables

List outputs and deliverables from the process as a whole and their destination

> - Project charter
> - Minutes from start-up meeting
> - Project recorded in register

7. Roles & Responsibilities

Define the Process Owner and Process Manager. Expand on the roles and responsibilities of the people in the 'Who' column for the process as a whole if useful.

> The Project Owner owns the process instance
> The Project Manager manages the process, involving the Process Owner as necessary

Further Details

8. Customer Value

> Value to customers' businesses.
> For client projects, the definition of the project and application of resources

9. Measurements:

Process measurements, CSFs, KPIs and indicators applying on completion of the whole process

> Accuracy and usefulness of charter over time

10. Issues

E.g., biased business case; premature initiation; political influence, etc.

11 Constraints

Total funding, resources, management time available to projects

12. Further workflow details

13. Systems

Describe information systems, knowledge bases, databases and other IT or business systems support for the process.

Project Management System

14. Relevant documents

Provide hotlinks to documents that will assist in explaining this process overall, do not include those attached to process elements in the workflow matrix.

15. Resources

List items used to create the product or service that are not cited as inputs: e.g., XYZ machine; 123 equipment, abc method

16. Comments

Further information to aid understanding

17. Process Trigger

Project approved and project manager appointed by the sponsor

18. Completion

Kick-off meeting

19. Connecting customer processes

Supplier appointment; internal project team resource assignment

20. Control Mechanisms

Project Management System Summary Report

APPENDIX F

Subprocess Activity Template

Subprocess/Activity Profile

Name:		Code:	Responsibility:	
Part of process:		Level:	Process Manager:	
Information Needs:	Performance Measures:	Objectives:	Customer Value:	
			Critical Success Factors:	
Trigger:	Inputs:	Deliverables:	Completion	
Information Outputs:				
Version:	Issue Date:	Complied by:	Circulation Group:	

271

Activity Profile

Activity	
Screen	
Est. work time	
Performer	
Trigger	
Availability	
Input information	
Method	
Business rules	
Outputs	
Reminder/ Escalation/ Reassignment	
Constraints	

'Screen' and 'Performer' information may be filled in later.

'Trigger' defines the action or condition that tells the system when to start this activity.

'Availability' means when the activity is available to the user.

'Method' is the story for that activity.

GLOSSARY

ABC	Activity-Based Costing – a technique for costing processes and products/services.
ABM	Activity-Based Management – a technique using snapshot activity based costing to surface improvement hypotheses that are tested and implemented.
Activity	Work resulting in a change of state or an interim output.
Adaptive, adaptation	Reacting to changes.
Anti-fragility	The property of an organisation that can easily cope with unexpected events.
AS IS	Description or model of the current state, compare with TO BE.
Automated System	A system that progresses without human intervention, making decisions according to pre-specified rules.
BPM	Business Process Management – managing processes in a business, tends to refer to business process change programs and projects.
BPMN	Business Process Modelling and Notation – IT industry standard set of symbols for workflow charting business requirements for IT implementation using BPMS.
BPMS	BPM System – the IT tool or application (suite) used to implement and automate business processes.
BPR	Business Process Re-engineering – a popular means of saving costs in the 1990s that fell into disrepute.
BTE	Business Transformation Executive – a role that encompasses change and process management.

Business Requirements	Detailed description of business needs that can be used by IT to configure or code the software application.
Business Rule	The statement of a prior decision as to what is to happen at a decision point, depending up information available at the decision point, so a process can be automated.
Change Management	The management of organisational change, particularly with reference to people and the impact of change upon them.
CIO	Chief Information Officer
Collaboration	Working together for mutual advantage.
Complexity	To be of such sophistication in form or content that predictability is not possible.
Complexity Theory	Approaches that recognise complexity and its form and suggest ways of understanding and dealing with it.
COO	Chief Operating Officer
CPO	Chief Process Officer
Critical path	The shortest route through a system or set of activities necessary to achieve an output or outcome.
CRM	Customer Relationship Management – a computer system for managing customer information.
Cycle Time	The total time taken from the beginning to the end of a process.
Decision Point	Where workflow branches into alternative paths and a decision is required as to which path to take.
De-layering	Reducing the number of organisational levels.
Deliverable	A tangible, measurable, output from an activity, process, etc.
Duration	Time taken to complete a part of a process—typically an activity, but could be a subprocess or task.

Dwell Time (aka lag or dead time)	Unproductive waiting time before work commences.
EAI	Enterprise Applications Integration – computer systems that link other computer systems.
EPO	Enterprise Program Office – part of the CEO's office responsible for providing support, tools and methods to programs.
eBusiness	Business transactions conducted within and between organisations using internet technology.
eCommerce	Buying/selling transactions conducted over the internet between buyers and sellers often unknown to each other.
ERP	Enterprise Resource Planning – an enterprise computer system for the management of many aspects of a business.
Evolution	Long-term permanent adaptation to suit the changing environment.
Exogenous Factor	Something external to a system that is applied to leverage a change to a system.
Flow Chart	A diagram showing the linked progression of the activities that make up a process.
Fragility	The risk of an organisation being detrimentally impacted by a significant unexpected event.
Function(al)	Relating to a specialised part of an organisation that only works on activities requiring that speciality.
Go-Live	The moment at which a new process and system start operating and the previous process is withdrawn.
Governance	The means of directing and managing an enterprise for the benefit of specified stakeholders.
iBPMS	Intelligent BPMS – can handle case management, big data analysis and other more advanced BPMS functions.

ISO 9000	An internationally recognised and audited quality standard.
Key (Business) Process	One of a limited number of strategic business process categories on the top level of a process architecture. Processes are the next level down.
KPI	Key Performance Indicator.
Leverage Point	The point where the application of pressure or resource to a system will have an intended effect on the system.
Outcome	The eventual manifested result.
Permeable	A barrier that allows certain elements through, such as water or information.
PMO	Project Management Office – responsible for providing support, tools and methods to projects.
PMG	Program Management Group – the working group for the program comprising stakeholder managers, the BPM Specialist or Consultant and the Program Manager.
Procedure	A process tailored to a particular organisation, containing actual organisational roles and data.
Process	A series of end-to-end related activities that result in an outcome or output of value to the customer.
Process Architecture	All processes in an organisation depicted to show the lateral and vertical relationships with each other.
Process Chart or Map	A diagrammatic representation of a process.
Process Deconstruction Diagram	A diagram representing the relationship between two process levels.
Process Re-engineering	Fundamentally changing a process by designing from scratch again.

RFID	Radio Frequency Identification – small, cheap, solid state devices attached to goods to enable them to be identified and located.
Robustness	The attribute an organisation needs to be able to combat the adverse impact of unexpected events.
Roll Out	The implementation sequence.
Silo	Used to denote how a part of an organisation, typically a function, can become isolated from other parts of the organisation.
Six Sigma	A disciplined and extreme, data-driven approach and methodology for eliminating defects in any process.
SMG	Stakeholder Management Group – the steering committee for the program, comprising senior executive stakeholders.
SOA	Service Oriented Architecture – an IT systems modular architecture approach intended to better support business processes.
Sponsor	A person who can provide funding, influence or power to a process, project or other activity by associating with it.
Stakeholder	Any person or group with an interest.
Straight-through processing	Computer-based automatic progression of a process without human intervention.
Subprocess	A level below the process level and above the activity level that brings together groups of activities into phases within a process.
Subsidiarity	Making everyone focus on supporting the group dealing with the constraint.
Subordinating	Directing effort to removing the constraint.
Swim Lanes	A diagrammatic technique that shows different organisational units, one per 'lane' or column.
SYSTEM	TO BE process design optimised to use workflow (BPMS) technology.

Systems Thinking	A well-developed body of approaches that emphasise the totality of a system rather than its components.
Task	A technical piece of work undertaken by a person or team. A number of tasks make up a process activity.
Theory of Constraints	A sub-set of systems thinking that deals with how to optimise a system by focusing on the system constraint.
Tipping Point	When a system tips from one stable dynamic state to a new, different, stable dynamic state.
TO BE	A model of a process according to a new design.
TQM	Total Quality Management – an approach directed at achieving as close to perfect output as possible by managing processes.
Trigger	An event or condition that is the signal to start a process or activity.
Upstream	Closer to the customer.
Value	Has a use or intrinsic worth to the recipient.
Value Chain	A series of activities that create and build value.
Value Proposition	A statement explaining how value will be created and what it will enable the customer to do in their business.
Value Stream	A value chain for a single line of business.
WIIFM	'What's in it for me' – a statement of value to an individual.
Workflow	A series of linked work activities.
Y2K	Year 2000 – relating to an expectation that computer systems had to be altered leading up to 01/01/2000 to prevent program breakdowns—which largely did not happen.

REFERENCES

[i]   Thomas Davenport. Appears in 53 books from 1976–2008

[ii]   Michael Hammer, *The Agenda*, Random House, 2001

[iii]   Peter M. Senge, *The Fifth Discipline*, Doubleday/Currency, 1990

[iv]   Peter Senge et al, *The Fifth Discipline Fieldbook*, Nicholas Brealey Publishing, 1994

[v]   For more about TOC refer to books by Eliyahu Goldratt published by North River Press

[vi]   Fritjof Capra, *The Web of Life*, Flamingo/Harper Collins, 1996

[vii]   http://en.wikipedia.org/wiki/Uncertainty

[viii]   Richard Stoneham, *A Systems Framework For Complex Projects*, 2003; http://www.stratege.com.au/A Systems Framework for Complex Projects Overview.pdf

[ix]   http://en.wikipedia.org/wiki/Leadership

[x]   http://www.uky.edu/~gmswan3/575/KM_and_OL.pdf

[xi]   http://www.bqf.org.uk/efqm-excellence-model

[xii]   Baldrige Performance Excellence Program, *2013–2014 Criteria for Performance Excellence*, 2013, (Gaithersburg, MD: U.S. Department of Commerce, National Institute of Standards and Technology, http://www.nist.gov/baldrige/publications/business_nonprofit_criteria.cfm).

[xiii]   http://hbr.org/2007/04/the-process-audit/ar/1

[xiv]   Michael Porter, *Competitive Advantage*, Free Press, 1980

[xv]   *Seven Key Guidelines to BPM Project Success*, available on Gartner's website at http://www.gartner.com/resId=1254813

[xvi]   Acknowledgement to *Viable Metrics to Justify a BPM Project* by Kay Winkler + comments, Feb 2013 on BPMLeader.com

[xvii]   Reported in *Revisiting Reengineering*, Art Kleiner, strategy+business, Jul 2000

[xviii]   http://www.omg.org/spec/BPMN/2.0/PDF/

[xix]   Acknowledgement to *Viable Metrics to Justify a BPM Project* by Kay Winkler + comments, Feb 2013 on BPMLeader.com

[xx]   BizAgi, available free from www.bizagi.com

[xxi]   http://www.eclarus.com/resources/BPMN_Poster_A3_ver_1.0.9.pdf There are other sources that a search will reveal.

[xxii]   http://en.wikipedia.org/wiki/Data_modeling

xxiii Peter Senge et al, *The Fifth Discipline Fieldbook*, Nicholas Brealey Publishing, 1994; https://www.solonline.org/?tool_ladder_of_infer

xxiv http://gladwell.com/the-tipping-point/

xxv Nassim Nicholas Taleb, *Antifragile*, Allen Lane, 2012

xxvi Nassim Nicholas Taleb, *Fooled by Randomness*, Random House, 2001; *The Black Swan*, Random House, 2007.

xxvii Gary Hamel, *Bureaucracy Must Die*, HBR, 2014; https://hbr.org/2014/11/bureaucracy-must-die

INDEX